To: The Brighams —
   David Chamberlain says
you are a big fan of Rush
Limbaugh and might like this
book.
               All best,
                 Charley Dickey

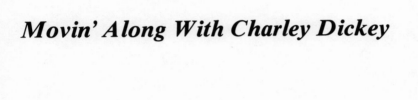

Movin' Along With Charley Dickey

Movin' Along With Charley Dickey

CHARLEY DICKEY
Illustrations by Joseph Fornelli

WINCHESTER PRESS

An Imprint of *NEW WIN PUBLISHING, INC.*

The publisher and author thank the following publications for graciously permitting the stories in this collection to be used. The stories first appeared in the magazines listed below.

Petersen's Hunting; "And Then What?" January, 1979; "Edited Dreams" August, 1983; "Magic Moment" October, 1983; "Reach Out and Punch Someone" June, 1976; "Avoidance Techniques" January, 1983; "A Matter of Timing" May, 1983; "A Nostalgic Whiff" August, 1984; "Early Training" April, 9184; Purdey Is As Purdey Does" September, 1984; "A Helping Hand" July, 1982; "Lines to Exit By" August, 1982; "Whether 'tis Nobler to Shoot" (originally appeared as "Turkey Hunting Ethics"), March, 1985; "The Long and Short of It" May, 1982; "Mister Willie" June, 1983; "Old Masters" November, 1982; "The Red Revival" April, 1982; "Clothes Don't Make the Hunter" March, 1982; "Deer Etiquette" January, 1984; "All He Wants for Christmas" December, 1984; "No Pain, No Game" June, 1982; "There's Always a Way" February, 1984; "The Good Ol' Boys" February, 1982; "I, Being of Sound Mind" May, 1984; "A Dog-Eat-Bird World" March, 1985

Petersen Hunting Annual: "Setting the Pace" Originally appeared as "The Longest Yard"). Winter, 1985.

Georgia Sportsman: "Up in Smoke" April, 1985; "Whippoorwon't" August, 1981; "Because They Are There" September, 1981; "Divine Intervention" May, 1983; "Bearing with Bruins" February, 1982; "Just One More Time" June, 1982; "Dial an Excuse" July, 1982; "A Tough Bottle to Crack" June, 1981; "By the Light of the Silvery Moon" March, 1985; "The Packrats" January, 1981; "Catch and Release" June, 1983; "Fishing Psychosis" August, 1983; "The Art Collector" February, 1981; "Midnight's Cowboy" March, 1981; "The Sport of Disorienteering" August, 1984; "The Old Equalizers" (originally appeared as "Dove Shooting Made Easy— Nearly") September, 1981; "The Awful Truth" July, 1984; "Never Say Diet" December, 1981; "Deceived by the Ringusdingus" January, 1983; "Parles-vous Fishing?" November 1983.

Outdoor Life Bass and Freshwater Fishing Annual: "It's Tough to be a Bass Fisherman"). 1985.

North American Whitetail: "All the Comforts of Deer Camp" (originally appeared as "Deer Camps Neat, Clean, and Otherwise). April, 1983; "Deer Mathematics" (originally appeared as "Of Buck Fever, Lying And Other Deer Hunting Maladies"), February, 1983.

Library of Congress Cataloging in Publication Data

Dickey, Charley.
    Movin' Along With Charley Dickey

Acknowledgments

My deepest thanks to the following people who have helped with this book in one way or another: Bunty Dickey, Tammi Wathen, Bob Elman, Frank Gil, Craig Boddington, Ken Elliott, Jeanne Frissell, Steve Vaughn, David Morris, Aaron Pass, Gordon Whittington, Red and Kathryn Chaplin, Tom Mann, Suzanne Newsom, Woody Earnheart, Ottie M. Snyder, Jr., Bill Mitzel, Tommy Holloway, Chris Christian, Jeann Sinclair, Neil Rogers, Mike Toth, Sally Antrobus, Jim Shepherd, and Bill McGrotha. My special appreciation to America's outdoorsmen who generously keep me supplied with material—whether or not they intend to. Errors in this book should be attributed to my wife Bunty; correct information should be credited to the author.

To Barbara Cooke Perrin

Table of Contents

Preface

Humor is a part of almost every outdoor trip. Later, the trip becomes nostalgia. Hunters, fishermen, and other outdoorsmen easily identify with the fun and mistakes of other sportsmen because they've been there. A sportsman in one region quickly relates to a story about a "character" in another area, because he knows someone just like him.

As a freelance outdoor writer, Charley Dickey usually writes humor, nostalgia, and narratives about the wonderful characters we all meet on the trail. He's written how-to and where-to for most of the outdoor magazines, but he's more interested in the people he hunts and fishes with than in the lures and bullets they use.

Dickey, who writes a weekly outdoor column for the *Tallahassee Democrat*, has been writing the back page of *Petersen's Hunting* under the pen name of Sam Cole since the magazine began publication 13 years ago. He also writes the back page each month for Game & Fish Publications' *Georgia Sportsman* and eight more magazines published by the company. For *North American Whitetail*, he writes a series of articles that relate the pranks and calamities of the 10 members of the "Trophy Buck and Fine Arts Society" and their guests. He also writes a regular column for *Tom Mann Outdoors*.

This is Dickey's seventh book. His writing career started at the age of nine when he sold his first article to a newspaper for $2.76. Later, he majored in natural science at the Universities of New Mexico and Tennessee. During World War II and the Korean conflict, he flew torpedo bombers from carriers.

Dickey has lived in New England, the Middle Atlantic States, the West Coast, and several parts of the South. He has hunted and fished in many countries, and the moving about has given him a wide background for his stories. While working with the sporting arms and ammunition industry for more than 20 years, he was privileged to meet many outdoorsmen, who provided a constant source of new material. In 1982, he was awarded the Outdoor Writers Association of America's Excellence of Craft Award, the highest the organization gives for photojournalism.

A native of Bulls Gap, Tennessee, Dickey now travels out of Tallahassee, Florida, to collect story material. His partner and wife Bunty, the former Barbara Goddard Theg, accompanies Dickey on many of his trips, such as a visit to Cuba five years ago when she was the tour group's only woman. They have three grown children, one grandchild, and a varying number of bird dogs.

Movin' Along With Charley Dickey

And Then What?

Throwing out the Christmas tree on New Year's Day is like telling an old hunting buddy goodby after spending several days with him at duck camp. No matter how clean the bathtub water, though, there comes a time when you have to pull the plug.

Things end and things start over. I am always a little sad on New Year's Day, not necessarily as a result of refreshments the night before. I have a Southern quail-hunting friend who has the quaint habit of eating turnip greens and black-eyed peas for breakfast on New Year's morning. Now, that's enough to make anyone sad!

He says it's a Southern tradition to consume such oddities because it brings good luck through the coming year. He mixes great heaps of fatback with the peas, keeps the pot bubbling, and nibbles on the strange mess through three straight football games.

I cannot argue with his custom. I don't understand how it brings him luck, but Rebs have unique systems for wooing or changing luck. All I know is that he has more coveys of bobwhite quail marked on a secret map than anyone south of Baltimore. Not only that, he can take you to each location on time—at the exact moment when the birds are there.

I have tried eating turnip greens and black-eyed peas to see if I could find more quail. It has not helped. Perhaps I should have fed the concoction to my dogs, assuming I could force them to eat it.

New Year's Day is a time to take personal inventory. Maybe that makes me a little sad, looking back and knowing another year has slipped by and I didn't take all of the grand hunting trips I had planned. My intentions were good, but too many things came up. There were good days afield, but there could have been many more.

Basically a man makes his own luck. If he doesn't plan trips, he probably won't go on many. I don't mean exotic trips to a foreign country but those near home or within a day's driving distance.

What's the point of working hard to make money if you don't spend part of it doing the things you like most? A new room for the house may not be as important as weekends in the field. Rather than trading for a new car, the money might better be spent at a hunting lodge.

One of my resolutions each New Year's Day is to spend more time in duck blinds, at deer camp, and with my bird dogs. I try to, but it never quite works out. One of Charley's principles is that a man is fortunate to hunt half as much as he plans.

I never can beat the principle even though I plan my oral surgery, hernias, and slipped disks for summer. I volunteer for jury duty in the spring so they won't summon me in the fall. I go to see my lawyer, banker, and preacher in July to head off problems that might explode in autumn.

My vacations are always planned for fall. I tell my relatives not to visit during the hunting season and, if they are going to die, to try and make it spring or summer. I try to save a few bucks and ask the kids not to write home for money between September and March.

On New Year's Day I think a lot about hunting and how I can go more often in the coming year. Yet unexpected emergencies always seem to happen during the hunting season. What I really need is a job where I work hard seven months a year and am free to hunt the other five months.

I envy people such as Lax Talbott out near Butte, Montana. Few people know that he used to be an economics professor. Lax guides deer and elk hunters in the fall. Or rather, he goes hunting and lets them come along for a fee. In the summer, he goes trout fishing in the Big Hole, and if some dude wants to learn how to raise a brown trout on a dry fly, Lax lets him tag behind.

I've followed Lax a few times and, one night after deer liver and onions, I asked him how he possibly made enough money on which to live. Lax, poking his knife at a balky sinew wedged between molars, gave a long sigh. Then he slowly explained that a man has to have a sense of values and a system of priorities. Somewhere in life, he has to decide what he really wants to do: He has to be practical about it and willing to pay the price.

Then he told me his "And Then What?" story about the national sales manager of a big corporation in New York who flew out each year for a week of elk hunting. The sales manager was always exhausted when he arrived, but by the second day he was a new man. His color came back and his eyes cleared. His nerves settled and he quit reaching for imaginary telephones. He only lit one cigarette at a time.

The sales manager raved at the beauty of the country, marveled at the peace, and relaxed in the quiet. He took a great fancy to Lax and said, "With your easy-going personality, you ought to go to work for me. Everybody would like you, and you'd be able to outsell anyone in the company."

Lax said, "And then what?"

The sales manager replied, "You'd soon be getting bonuses and move up to be a district manager, maybe Dallas or Chicago."

Lax asked, "And then what?"

"You'd make more money in a month than you make all year out here. You'd get promoted to regional manager and have stock options."

"And then what?"

"Well, eventually you'd come back to New York, be my assistant sales manager, and travel all over the country. You'd have a big home in the suburbs, an apartment in the city, and a wallet full of credit cards."

Lax mumbled, "And then what?"

The excited sales manager shouted, "The best of all! Whenever you could squeeze some time off, you could fly out here and go hunting for a week!"

Well, Lax is still in Montana. He has HIS priorities straight!

Edited Dreams

Most of the time my two English setters sleep quietly. But sometimes the older dog works all four legs in his sleep as though he's chasing something. He yips lightly and once in a while he quivers. If he becomes too agitated in his dreams, I nudge him gently and he relaxes back into a deep sleep.

I wonder what he dreams about. I have never seen him go on point while slumbering, although he can be quite stylish while pointing a covey of quail. It pains me to think that he might dream of chasing deer, one of his fondest desires and a compulsion that has caused me considerable embarrassment and much extra training time.

Sometimes when I wake him from dreamy agitation, he raises his head, looks guilty for a moment, and then puts his head back down. In a few seconds, he is twitching again, as if he's picked up the same dream, maybe the same deer.

Perhaps I am too suspicious of his past sins and he is really dreaming of pointing huge coveys of quail. He might even be dreaming of perfect dog behavior in the field, though I think that's unlikely. Whatever his dreams, I hope they are pleasant ones. I don't care how much he dreams of chasing deer or cottontails as long as it doesn't carry over into his hunting time.

I do not care much for dreaming. Unless I immediately write down what I was dreaming about when awakening, I'll quickly forget all details. All that will be remembered was whether it was a good dream or a bad one.

It is more pleasant to daydream. After a full dinner of squirrel stew, when you have had one more helping then you needed, it is heavenly to lie back in a leather lounge chair, loosen your belt, and let your mind conjure up some pleasant thoughts. You slowly drift into the half world, where you are neither alertly awake nor asleep. You are relaxed enough for your subconscious mind to start rolling a printout of memories. Your conscious mind has a bit of control, but if you use it the computer tape from your memory storage will not flow freely.

There is a delicate balance, a hypnotic trance when there is a free flow of details you had not consciously remembered for a long time. When all the conditions are in harmony, I can replay the scene of more than half a century ago when I shot my first mourning dove. I remember all the details of that first shotgun I owned, a .410 single shot with a big hammer and light paisley blueing on the receiver.

The grownups put me off in a corner of a harvested cornfield by myself. Although I had been checked out in the basics of safety, I had missed the lessons on sportsmanship. When a dove landed in a nearby pine tree, I took rifle aim and dropped the bird off the limb. I quickly ran to the dove, picked it up, and propped my shotgun against the tree. Then I went running down the field to show everyone my trophy.

I had been so busy concentrating on my shooting and retrieving that I had not heard the whoops of laughter. As I approached the nearest stand, proudly holding high the first dove of the shoot, Uncle Whit stepped out of the weeds, smiled at me, and asked, "Didn't anybody tell you, boy, you're supposed to shoot doves while they're flying?"

"No sir," I replied. "I thought you were supposed to shoot them anyway you could."

Uncle Whit, who wasn't my real uncle, but sort of an uncle to everybody in town, reached out and ruffled my hair. "Don't pay any attention to that laughing. You needed to get one to get your confidence up. Now go back and shoot the rest flying. Shoot way ahead of them."

I nearly shot all my shells before I finally connected with one. The bird's feet were down and it was inches from landing in that pine tree, but at least it was flying. That's when Uncle Whit left his stand and came down to give me some coaching. With Uncle Whit standing behind me talking soft and gentle, I cut a couple of tail feathers. Then, with my last shell, I centered a dove that was flying wide open across the field.

I was so proud and excited that I promised to mow Uncle Whit's yard free for the rest of his life. He just smiled and said, "You keep leading those doves. I don't need any mowing." I'd forgotten that Uncle Whit was too busy hunting and fishing to ever plant any grass.

Maybe I can recall that day so easily because I humiliated myself in front of those grownups. Or my memory got an extra deep imprint because it was my first dove and first wingshooting.

One of my favorite replays is the time I got a triple on black ducks near Chincoteague several years ago when the daily limit was a little more generous. I was hunting the opening day with Ira Walby, who always takes 30 minutes longer to arrange his decoys than anybody else I know.

I can clearly see it now. Ira was pouring coffee and had both hands full when six blacks came straight in out of the mist. There was a time when I could recall getting only two, but now I remember how I quickly took the front duck, shucked the Model 12, collapsed a swerving black, and then knocked down the third one as it climbed. The memory is as vivid as if it happened only a minute ago.

I replay this memory often when I'm relaxing. You don't get a triple on blacks every day, and now I couldn't shuck a pump fast enough to bag a triple if the ducks threw out sky anchors and parked over the decoys. Just recently I was having coffee with Ira down at the Sportsman's Diner and I asked him if he still remembered that Chincoteague triple.

Ira gave me a funny look and said, "Strange that you should mention that particular trip. I was reading about it in my diary last night. And my records show you didn't hit a duck. You getting senile or something?"

Well, I never did think much of Ira Walby. To begin with, he comes from poor stock. I can't understand why I've hunted with him all these years.

One thing's for sure: I'm not going to let some fool diary mess up my dreams!

Up in Smoke

Sandy Gilpin blamed me for getting him hooked again on cigarettes. Before it was all over, I nearly lost one of my best fishing buddies. I'd like to know, though, what you'd have done under my circumstances.

It's liable to happen to anyone. Its most severe form in deer hunting occurs just as the patient sees or hears deer—buck fever. There are also aftershocks. With fishing, the delirium sets in right after a sudden and unexpectedly large fish is landed.

Very few anglers actually die from fish shock. They just give most of the main symptoms and indications, enough of them so that you feel guilty for wondering who is mentioned in their wills to get the best rods.

An angler suffering from fish trauma is more likely to frighten his companion to death than to expire himself. For instance, a typical symptom of fish terrors' is succussion, the act or process of shaking violently. When an afflicted angler is in the full force of this vibrator, one is not sure if he will disintegrate or have a stroke. After all, there's no way that we laymen can know how securely an angler is wired. He may have more loose connections than we ever suspected.

I don't like to think it may be a stroke because I can't remember whether I prop his head up, his feet up, or simply throw him overboard. It's not easy to remember whether I should wrap a blanket around him, which is never aboard any vessel I fish on, or try to revive him with cold water.

Most freshwater fishing is done from small boats. It's easy to lean over the gunwale and douse water on the patient. That's what I usually do, but I don't have a lot of confidence in it being the right procedure. It's the same feeling you get when you're walking a topwater plug and an inner voice is saying you should be bumping the bottom with a worm.

I never get fish tremors while I am fishing. Let's say my buddy and I are casting for two-pound fish. Suddenly my lure is attacked by an eight-pound fish! In all modesty, I play the lunker fairly calmly. One reason is that I don't believe I'm going to land him in the first place. It is exactly the correct time for the tensile strength of something to give up, such as on the line, hooks, drag, or anchor line. Also, if my buddy is fated to make a mistake that month, he will make it during the landing of that fish. In fact, the moths probably finished eating the bottom of the net for dinner the night before.

If the fish, by great good fortune, is boated, I will remain calm while the lure is removed, the fish is briefly admired, and then is dropped in the live well. After I inspect the hatch on the live well and make sure the compartment won't flop out of the boat, I collapse on a seat. Then the earthquake of tremors starts through my body. It begins with a slow bubble of electrical shocks and quickly works its way up to about 9.8 on the Richter scale. At 10 you atomize.

I always feel guilty when these uncontrollable tremors flow through me. After all, I'm a grown man and all I did was catch an exceptional fish. Then I go in and out of hallucinations, delusions, and incoherence. A witness once accused me of speaking in unknown tongues. I didn't put much stock in that because he's always getting his hearing aid wires crossed.

Once an angler goes into aftershock, there is no way of predicting how long he will remain in that condition. For all of them, especially those who become rigid, I feel that in the name of human kindness I should try to do something for them. Because their hands are incapable of holding a rod and reel, I go ahead and fish and hope that God's fresh air and sun will help them. If they are deep in a hallucination, I figure this is a good time to fish their favorite spots without their knowing.

This gives me a chance to get in more fishing from the front of the boat. Sometimes, of course, it's hard work to move a heavy angler from the front to the back while he's in a comatose condition.

Sandy Gilpin, who's an experienced angler, didn't go into Never-Never Land when he accidentally landed a huge bass. He just sat there shaking. With a deer hunter under the affliction, the first thing you do is take his gun. So I removed Sandy's rod and reel and tackle box. If he fell over, I didn't want him to get impaled on a treble hook.

After a couple minutes, the whole boat began to vibrate. It got so bad I went back and checked the clamps on the motor mount. Sandy's eyes were glazed, he was slapping his pockets, and he was trying to tell me something. It was obvious that I had to administer some sort of first aid.

I threw a handful of water on his face but that only made him mumble louder. He kept pounding his pants and shirt pockets. Then I realized that Sandy wanted a cigarette.

I went through all his pockets but couldn't find any. Because I haven't smoked in years, there wasn't a butt on board. I hadn't seen Sandy smoke all morning. Then I thought of his tackle box!

There was half a pack and a lighter hidden in a plastic bag of grape worms. I took one of the cigarettes and tried to shove it between Sandy's lips. His teeth were clenched and he was mumbling louder than before. In desperation, I gave him a karate chop on the nape of the neck. When his mouth flew open, I jammed the cigarette in. I flicked the lighter and yelled. "Draw, Sandy, draw!"

He kept mumbling. I inserted two more cigarettes and sparked them. Sandy's coloring started coming back. He finished the pack before we got back to the ramp.

I stopped by to see Sandy that night and he wouldn't speak to me and neither would his wife. They were hopping mad, and both said I got him back on the cigarette addiction after he'd quit.

Well, after you save a man's life you don't expect that kind of welcome. I pointed out that the cigarettes were in Sandy's box with the lighter and that I didn't smoke. "Tell me," I said, "when did you kick smoking?"

Sandy stood up proudly, jutted his chin and gritted, "I had been quit for two days until you got me started back."

Whippoorwon't

One of the things that makes camping difficult is whippoorwills. Its favorite habitat, or that of its cousin the chuckwill's widow, is the tree nearest your tent.

The main hobby of the whipppoorwill is keeping honest sportsmen awake all night. The bird gets its name from the nocturnal or crepuscular call it makes. When they get wound up, they repeat the same shrill cry over and over.

The brown birds are limited in their musical repertoire, and that's another of the things that makes them objectionable. A whippoorwill whistles *whip-poor-will* at the rate of 60 times a minute.

No matter what time you climb into your sack, that's when a whippor-will cranks up. There is no melody at all in the call. It is a shrill, demanding commercial, much like those trying to sell you a used car on television. It is more advertising than a small bird needs, and certainly more than anyone who is trying to doze off can stand.

The whippoorwill has little fear of man. It is protected by law and takes advantage of the fact. They have a tendency to return to the same ancient nesting area each spring and use the same limb, or spot on the ground, for a shot at the world record for most consecutive calls. On a recent fishing trip with my wife, our tent was pegged into the social center of an ancient calling ground and depot for any migrating whippoorwills.

On the first night of our trip, I had no sooner gotten my feet comfortable in the bedroll than a whippoorwill landed on the main bracing pole of our tent. It's like having a broken record with three notes playing at the head of your bed.

While it may be of help to count sheep while trying to get to sleep, I always select sheep that don't bleat. The whippoorwill had a trial run of five minutes of whistles, about 302 as I counted them. Then there was complete silence, and I thought perhaps the bird had flown.

Wondering, however, when the bird would start up again was as maddening as listening to him. It's like listening to a distant barking dog in a kennel at night. Once you get your mind set on the barking, and you're really concentrating on it, the silences are as disturbing as the barking. You keep wondering when the dog will start up again.

Finally, just as I was dozing into a dream of a big fish on the morrow, the salesman got his second wind. I eased one arm out of the sleeping bag, felt in the dark until I found one of my wife's boots, and heaved it at the top of the stake. The distance was short and my accuracy was good. The immediate problem was that there was a layer of tenting between the bird and the boot. It ricocheted off the canvas and collided with my wife's posterior. She rolled over and sat up in a rather quick motion and screamed, "What's going on, Buster?"

"Surely you jest," I said. "You couldn't have been sleeping with that crazy bird whistling at us?"

"What bird?" she asked.

If there's one thing I know about whippoorwills, it's that they are stubborn. Once a bird gets his mind set on using a particular peg or limb to advertise from, he's going to use it all night. There can be a thousand limbs in the forest just like it, but he has to have that one.

I fumbled around in the dark until I found my flashlight, and then located three candles in the emergency first aid box. I put on my boots and crawled out into the darkness in my underwear. My wife began laughing.

"What's so funny?" I shouted.

"Oh, in the beam of light you look so funny in your boots and skivvies. Are you going to do a strip tease?"

"Go ahead," I yelled. "Crack jokes while I'm trying to save your sanity."

I noticed that lights in the surrounding tents were popping on and their beams waving around wildly as some of the occupants were trying to slide into britches. It didn't slow me. No idiotic whippoorwill was going to use my tent poles for a singing ground. I lit the first candle and waxed it to the front pole, which protruded through the top a few inches. Then, I put candles on the other two main braces and lit the wicks.

As I climbed inside, my wife said, "You're going to burn us alive!"

"I don't care if I do," I shouted. "It's better than being tortured to death by a bird saying the same thing over and over."

It was impossible to go to sleep. The whippoorwill had come back and landed in an oak limb that hung above our tent. Deciding to be calm and indifferent about the whole affair, I let the bird reach 724 straight calls before I ran outside.

I grabbed the small ax by the dead campfire and rushed to the tree. By swinging it carefully in short strokes, I could safely cut the base of the limb the whippoorwill was whistling on. Just as the limb crashed into my tent, a delegation arrived. The law enforcement officers were led by the campground owner and a couple of little old ladies in tennis shoes.

Before the deputies took me to town, I looked back at the oak tree. The whippoorwill was perched on the next limb up and whistling to a constant 60-per-minute rate. "*I told you so! I told you so!*" I turned toward my wife. She was whistling in perfect harmony. "I told you so!"

Magic Moment

October should be all of the time! October is yellows and reds and russets stitched with evergreens against a blue sky cleared by great masses of crisp air washing the continent. It's color time. Whether you prefer New England maples, Missouri hickories, or Utah aspens, your favorite colors glisten in the sun as the leaves play a wind's tune.

Great things are about to happen, hunts you have planned for long months. There's a smell of gun oil and leather, and the dogs dance on their hind legs when they see you coming.

The air tingles with promise. There are memories of many hunts, not just those recorded in the brain, but feelings and senses that have seeped deep inside and become a part of you. There are old longings and new vibrations that you haven't felt for too many days. October brings these things back, and quickly, too. It is as though they were never away.

You remember your first gun and your first hunt. Perhaps the best day was when your dad let you hunt by yourself for part or all of a hunt. Maybe he left you alone before dawn to sit watching a hickory tree for squirrels, or put you in a duck blind by yourself for the first time, or trusted you to stay on stand at a dove field and not shoot low.

It was a grand moment, one you had waited and hoped for. It meant that you could be trusted with a gun, that you had learned to respect the other hunters and the game, and that you had confidence in yourself. It was also a frightening moment. There was so much to remember and you wanted to do well so you would be accepted as a hunter.

Suddenly you had to make the decisions. There was no one to tell you when a dove was in range, to hold off until the ducks came a little closer, or not to raise your .22 rifle until the squirrel was looking another way. Suppose you had an easy shot and missed? Or you didn't bag anything all day?

It is fine for fathers to tell their sons that they can have a good time hunting whether they bag anything or not. That is what the sons will say to their boys later in life. When you are a small boy on your first hunt alone, though, you find yourself praying that you bag something, even an ancient squirrel with gout.

Hunting on your own for the first time is more difficult than a test in school. With the school test, you have time to think; you can change your mind and erase. With a dove suddenly darting right over you, and nearly taking your cap off, there's no time to think. You get a quick chance and that's it. There's no second-guessing.

If you do poorly in school one day, you can pull your average up by doing better the next day. It's different with hunting. You get a day and then, too quickly, it is gone forever. What you do is what you did.

There is more inner pressure on you during that first hunt than during the test in school. There's a very simple reason for it. You would rather do a good job of hunting than make a top mark on a test.

You are on your own. You got yourself in this position because you always wanted to be a hunter. There's nothing for it but to grit your teeth, buckle down, and do your best. You remember the story of the little train trying to get up the hill, saying, "I think I can, I think I can, I *know* I can."

You open the gun as quietly as you can for the fortieth time to be sure the chamber is loaded. You check the safety over and over to be sure the gun is on safe, despite the fact that your right forefinger has been lightly riding it and you know you haven't moved the crossbolt.

It seems that you have been waiting for hours and no game has come. Perhaps you have an unlucky spot. You carefully take a look at your Mickey Mouse wristwatch. In one more minute, you will have been on station five minutes.

You try to remember all of your lessons and slowly keep swiveling your head to watch and listen for game. A duck hurtles out of the morning mist, crosses your blind, and disappears before you decide it was a duck. Where did it come from and how did it get by so fast? Perhaps the duck will return and give you a second chance.

Or, as you sit watching for a hungry squirrel, you hear the rustle of leaves behind you. It gets closer and closer, bearing down on you like a freight train. You know that if you turn, you'll spook the squirrel and you'll get a dodging, scampering shot by the time you get the rifle mounted. You should sit quietly and let the squirrel work past you toward the hickory tree. You can't stand it any longer, though. You have to look!

You quickly rise to your knees, twist your body, and at the same time bring the rifle to your cheek as you click the safety off. A brown thrush stares at you, wonders what you are up to, gives a hop, skip, and flies away. You can feel your heart racing and there is excitement in your throat. If the thrush had been a squirrel, you would have gotten it. You would have, you tell yourself, if the squirrel had stood there like the thrush. You sit back down, but not before looking around to make sure no silent hunter has seen your debacle.

Good things can happen on October mornings, too. Finally, a duck hovers over the decoys, a dove circles close in without seeing you, or a squirrel sits on a limb to inspect a hickory nut before whittling it. There is time and you put it all together. There is a plop or thud. You sit for an instant, unable to believe it. Then you put your gun down safely and race for your trophy. Its the best trophy you'll ever collect.

A long time later, and perhaps after more shots and even more game, you hear your dad blowing the car horn. You carefully unload your gun, grab your trophy, and run. You know you are not supposed to run with a gun in your hand, but you can't wait to show your success. Just before you break out of the woods onto a dirt road, you slow to a fast walk.

Your dad is standing by his old car, leaning against it with a foot backed up against the bumper. You're careful to point the gun muzzle straight down and, with your other hand, you hold your trophy high. A broad smile breaks out on your dad's face and you can see the speck of sun filtering through the yellow leaves like little searchlights on your dad's hunting coat.

Maybe some October it will occur to you that at that magic moment your dad was happier than you were, if that's possible.

Because They are There

My wife refers to autumn as the annual grunting season. You hunt squirrels from dawn until noon, then stop by home and switch your rifle for a fishing rod. If anyone asks you a question, you grunt.

When you get home at 10 p.m., you know you'll have to get to sleep fast to get six hours in before it's time to go hunting again. If your wife asks any questions while you're eating a warmed-over dinner, you grunt. She tells you good night and you grunt.

My wife says she can tell when a rainy front is going to move in. The grunt changes to a long sigh. If it rains more than one day the bags under my eyes almost clear up.

I have never been successful in explaining to her why I can jump out of bed with great vigor to go hunting at 4 a.m. but must be rolled out of bed and bounced on the floor to wake up on work days.

"It's different," I say. "That's all. It's just different."

Last year, during the autumnal endurance period, my wife asked why I had to both hunt and fish on the same day. I gave the question considerable thought. I wanted to come up with a logical and truthful answer that anyone could understand.

I said, "Because they are there."

It obviously wasn't the answer she expected. I could tell that by the way she ran screaming from the room. When a famous mountain climber said he scaled a stratospheric peak simply because it was there, though, the whole world accepted his answer. In fact, he became even more of a hero.

Why? In the first place, there was no sense to his answer. The climber had to be a bit sprung. Everybody realizes there's no hunting or fishing on top of the Himalayas. Of course, you might find the Abominable Snowman, but no one knows if it is legal to catch him or if the snowman will catch you!

It is much more logical to say that squirrels and bass are there, as I did. I wanted to acquire some of them because they were there. If they were not there, I wouldn't be interested in them at all.

During the autumnal period, my wife often says, "But you don't need another bass or squirrel."

"Yes I do!" I shout.

"Why?" she asks.

"Because."

"That's no answer."

"Well, then," I reply, "just because."

"You can come up with a better answer than that."

"If you must know," I say, "it's to satisfy deep emotional needs."

"You could satisfy your emotional requirements by cleaning the yard. How about trimming a few bushes so that visitors could find our home?"

"I'm leaving those bushes for songbirds. You can create a lot of wildlife habitat that way."

"Look," she says, "those bushes are so thick that birds are afraid to fly into them. The only kind of wildlife you've attracted is bats in the chimney."

"It's the wrong time of year for yard work," I reply.

"Why ?" she asks.

"Because the squirrel season only stays open so long and pretty soon it'll be too cold to fish. The yard stays right where it is all year and can be cleaned any old time."

She shouts, "That answer doesn't meet my emotional needs!"

"Well, I'll work on the yard next month."

"But, that's when some other hunting season will open and the water will get just right for some other kind of fish."

"Well, you can't expect the game and fish commission to set the season by when yards need a little tidying," I retorted.

" A little tidying!" she yelled. "There's no telling how many neighbors' kids have strayed into our yard and never been seen again."

"Well, with autumn coming on, the grass is going to die anyway. And, you know how raking leaves makes my old war wound hurt."

"What war wound?" she asks. "The only war wound you got was a busted ankle from slipping on a dance floor."

"Yeah, but if it had been overseas I might have gotten a Purple Heart. I knew. . . ."

"You're trying to change the subject. How is it you can walk up a trout stream or behind a bird dog all day and your ankle never acts up?"

"Well, you see, the cool mountain streams are healing."

"Yeah," she says, "and I suppose when you get tired hunting, you ride on the back of your bird dog?"

It sure is hard to get my wife's mind off a subject once she gets started. I could tell her I just inherited $1 million, and the first thing she'd ask is when I was going to get the leaves out of the gutter. I keep explaining that the rustic look gives character to our home, that we kind of blend into nature. That's the reason so many cars stop in front of our house and the occupants point and stare.

"Just answer me one thing!" she says. "Are you going to hunt squirrels and fish all fall?"

"It depends," I reply.

"On what?"

"If they are there!"

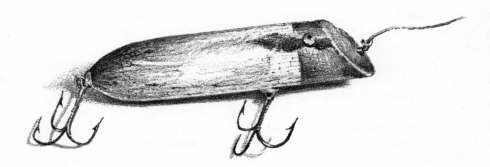

It's Tough to be a Bass Fisherman

I t's tough to be a bass fisherman, but somebody has to do it. Someone has to fish the rivers and lakes to keep them in balance.

It's even harder for bass guides and anglers to stay in some reasonable balance. Something always happens to disrupt the harmony. Even when nothing happens—such as no bass being caught—trouble tends to erupt between the two.

For their mutual welfare, the guide and his client should be a cooperative team allied against the fish. Too often though, the fisherman and his guide end up fighting one another; if not with fists, then at least with prolonged pouting.

Before the guide and angler ever meet, there are several things stewing that work against a happy relationship. It is the nature of any fisherman who spends his time and money on a distant trip to build up in his mind that he's going to catch something special, or a whole stringer of specials. If he so much as crosses his county border, he expects to return with several trophy bass iced down for the taxidermist. In fact, while planning his trip, he may ask his wife where she'd like to have the bass hung.

The angler expects his guide to show him secret hotspots clogged with huge bass. He glories in visions of having a professional teach him new ways to catch bass. He will return home with those techniques, become a local fishing legend, and never reveal a single secret to his best buddy. That's what he builds up in his mind. The truth of the matter is that he'd catch more bass if he stayed home and fished the waters he already knows.

Before the client arrives, the guides prays that he will be able to put the angler on stacks of bass gasping from hunger. He is fully aware of the fact that if the customer catches a trophy bass or a lot of medium size fish, there will be a generous tip. The guide also knows that his best advertising is from satisfied customers.

The guide is also firmly convinced that he knows more about fishing than the customer. In fact, the guide is pretty sure that the customer doesn't know much of anything, which may be right.

Being a guide is tough because he has to put up with any angler who comes along and has enough money to hire his services. Guiding requires great patience, but it beats getting a job and doing regular work. Guides revel in their positions of authority. They are looked up to as experts and the customers give them the benefit of the doubt, at least for the first hour or so.

It is fine for a guide to be an authority on catching bass. That's why the client hires him. By renting an authority's time and services, there is the clear implication that the professor will put the student on huge schools of monster bass and, in addition, that the customer will learn considerable about fishing.

There is something insidious, however, about a guide always playing the role of authority. He gets to liking it too much. Power breeds a desire for more power, and power corrupts. The guide may very well catch bass at times, and even be able to prove it, but he may come to believe that he's an authority on everything else. He not only proclaims what the correct lure to tie on is, but he knows exactly what is wrong with the United Nations and is momentarily expecting a message from the President to join his cabinet and solve all the nation's problems.

The guide is going to tell the customer how to fish—whether the fisherman wants to fish that way or not. The guide usually warms up to this stage by telling the client that he brought the wrong tackle and lures.

I realize, of course, that a client can show up with the wrong gear. I've done it enough times. I once took light bass tackle and 10-pound-test line to a lake choked with brush piles and car bodies. I couldn't have pulled a bluegill out of that jungle with my gear. The guide let me use one of his surf rods with 30-pound-test line. His rig worked very well and I caught several big bowfin.

If I had been fishing a lake with no more underwater obstructions than a bathtub, though, he'd have insisted that I use his block and tackle. From past experiences, guides have learned that anglers are not as likely to mess up and lose a sizable bass on a derrick as they are with light tackle.

The only bass that counts to a guide is a bass in the boat. It doesn't matter much how the fish gets there. Guides are convinced that paying customers cannot have a good time unless bass are boated. Very few people will pay $100 a day to go boat riding and count birds. If the customer catches a trophy bass, he will drive home and tell everyone in town, not to mention people along the way, and the guide will get more customers. It also improves the guide's reputation at his base marina if his customer comes back with loads of bass. There are usually spectators at the marina waiting to look at dead fish—and many of them have cameras.

It never occurs to a guide that the customer might like to fight a bass on light tackle. The customer really may not care about killing some strange bass he never met before. In fact, the customer may even feel that he has the right to fish the way he prefers.

I once contacted a guide of high reputation on Lake Tohopekaliga in central Florida to inquire about three days of January fishing. I repeatedly explained on the telephone that I only wanted to fish with topwater plugs and that it didn't matter whether I caught a bass or not. I knew that the bass would be bedding and that other anglers would be catching them with plastic worms and shiners, but I didn't care.

The guide was most understanding and said that I could fish any way I wanted to. In order to be sure that everything was clear, I told him that I had certain pure and simple reasons for wanting to fish *my* way: I didn't care anything about bass, but I was queer for topwater plugs.

He spent most of the first day trying to talk me into using his tackle and fishing with plastic worms. I kept pounding and chugging the surface with topwater lures. The second morning, he tried to get me to use shiners. I refused and he spent the afternoon pouting and grinding his teeth. By noon of the third day, I hadn't caught a fish. The guide wasn't speaking to me, even though I explained that he was actually better off because I wasn't messing up his boat with sticky fish. Whenever I tried to balance on a gunwale to answer nature's call, he'd jam the throttle and try to throw me in the lake.

Late in the afternoon, I finally angered a four-pound, mentally deficient bass into striking, I kept a tight line, but was in no hurry to bring the fish to net. The guide was jumping up and down screaming. "Bring it in! Get it in!"

On the third jump, the bass hurled the plug back to me.

The guide, red in the face and choking with anger, yelled, "I told you to crank it in!"

I turned, gave him my widest smile, and said, "Oh, I never like to net a bass until I've gotten at least three jumps."

It was two hours before quitting time, but the guide cranked up the motor and ran it wide open all the way back to the dock. The way he was shaking his head, I was afraid that he would injure his neck. After we unloaded the boat, I paid him and gave him the most generous tip I've ever given anyone, including the minister who performed my marriage ceremony.

The guide counted the money, shook his sore neck some more, and handed me back the tip.

"Here," he said, "you'd better keep this. You'll need it the next time you see your shrink!"

That incident illustrates the big trouble between guides and their customers. Both have the same objective—to catch fish. The eternal commanding authorities, however, don't want us amateurs to fish the way we want to fish, even when we're paying our own money.

The trouble with guides is even more basic. Because they are omniscient on their home waters, they tend to handle every customer the same way. Guides have trouble catching on to the fact that each bass angler is an individual and wants to be treated that way.

There are about 20 million bass fishermen in the United States and each has his own peculiarities. In fact, I'd say that if there is one common characteristic among bass fishermen, it's that they are a rugged bunch of individualists, or worse.

An amateur bass fisherman may not know much, but he likes to think that he knows a little bit. You don't see the casino operators in Las Vegas telling a customer that he's pulling a slot-machine handle the wrong way and, on top of that, that he's playing the wrong row of slots in the wrong room on the wrong day.

However you look at the controversy between professional guides and amateur anglers, there are a lot more ding-a-ling amateurs. That may be only because there are so many more amateurs to start with. If you really sit down and think hard about it, a guide has to have some crossed wiring or he wouldn't be a guide in the first place. I've known some amateur anglers who I wouldn't take fishing in my boat even if they gave me the inside of Fort Knox.

Beaver Forehand is a smiling, patient, warm, *former* guide on Lake Jackson, a lake in the Florida Panhandle that used to cough up a lot of 10-pound bass. Beaver is now in a different line of work, a steady job where he gets a paycheck and fringe benefits. When he goes fishing these days, he goes by himself.

A lot of things, such as flaky fishermen, contributed to Beaver's change in occupation. One of the anglers who helped him make up his mind came down from Long Island, New York, to catch a trophy bass. Beaver had to explain that the reel crank was what wound in the line.

The customer tippled, not only at night, but at frequent intervals during the day. Beaver baited the hook with large shiners, cast them to bedding areas, and handed him the rod. On the first morning, the customer's cork took off and Beaver kept yelling for him to set the hook. Unfortunately, the angler was preoccupied with other thoughts, perhaps the cattle egrets walking the bank.

Beaver finally rushed to the front of the boat, grabbed the rod, and set the hook. Then he handed the customer the rod and told him about the reel handle again. The angler wound in some slack, stopped, lit a cigarette, and then cranked some more.

The bass must have been dying of old age when the Long Islander finally dragged it close to the boat. Beaver stretched far out and netted a 14+-pound bass, the largest ever caught from Beaver's guiding, and a pound larger than any bass Beaver had ever caught. The customer didn't have much to say about the fish except that it was time to go back to his room and do some more relaxing.

Although the angler had booked two more days, the next morning he decided to drive back home. Beaver helped him load his gear and the customer was about to drive off when Beaver asked, "Aren't you going to pick up your trophy bass? I have it all iced down for you."

"What bass?" the tippler replied.

He had no memory of catching the 14+-pound bass the day before, a lake record for the year and a size Beaver had dreamed of catching for years.

Recalling that day, Beaver still says, "I figured picking cotton was a better way to make a living than guiding bass fishermen."

I don't want to harshly criticize bass guides or bass fishermen because I don't need any nasty letters. Some of both are among my best friends, although I wouldn't want my sister to marry either type.

I was with a guide once in Louisianna about a month after the spawning season. It had been a slow morning. Neither of us had gotten a strike, but he had told me a lot of stories about how many big bass his customers of the week before had caught.

At about 1:45 p.m., the surface suddenly began churning with long, skinny, female bass feeding on minnows to fatten up from the stresses of breeding. I cast a silver spoon past a clump of boils, started my retrieve, and *wham*! I worked a 28-inch or so bass up to the boat and tried to hold on until the guide netted her.

When the guide didn't show up, I turned around to see if he had fallen overboard. He wasn't even looking my way. He was carefullly packing up the loose gear and getting ready to crank the motor.

When I suggested that he might give me a little help, he said that it was too late. He always quite fishing at 2 p.m., he stated, and we were already late getting back to the dock. I thought he was a little late in letting me know that he worked only an eight-hour shift.

Just as guides should treat each bass customer as an individual, and adapt their service to meet the desires of the man paying the bill, the angler should not judge all guides the same. Each guide is an individual. Just because one guide has a deficiency doesn't mean that all the others are afflicted.

It is not fair to expect to guarantee fish. No one can tell what the bass will do on a given day, not even the bass. The sportsman, in his relationship with guides, should be tolerant, fair, and objective. From my own experience, let me give you two examples.

A few years ago, John McClanahan was my guide for trophy bass in the Ocala National Forest in central Florida. We fished hard the first day with shiners, sirens, plastic worms, and plugs, but we never got a bump. It was the same the second day on two different ponds, John said that if my hind end could stand it, we'd stay out and fish that night.

There was a full moon near midnight and, as we rounded an island, John showed me a point 200 yards ahead. He had rolled a big bass just off that point three weeks earlier. He told me to tie on a black jitterbug but not to cast until he told me. Using only the paddle, John quietly scooted us toward the point.

When we got in position, he whispered, "Cast to the edge of the sawgrass. If a bass hits, it will be about 10 feet from the grass."

I managed to drop the jitterbug where he had said, without it landing in the grass. I started a steady retrieve and, when the plug was 10 feet from the grass, the surface exploded. The bass hooked itself and ran into the sawgrass while I was fumbling about. It jumped three times in the moonlight, its sides glistening, and we knew this was a trophy. I didn't faint and John netted the bass—an 11+-pounder, the largest I had ever caught.

The next day, we didn't catch another bass. As far as I'm concerned, though, John McClanahan is the greatest bass guide who ever lived. I think of him every time I look at the wall mount. In fact, I offered to deed my house to John.

On a trip to Lake Miramar, one of the Southern California lakes that has been stocked with the giant Florida subspecies of largemouth bass and that may provide a new world record, I contacted a local guide who we'll call Puddin' Head.

I tried to follow every detailed instruction that Puddin' Head commanded. He fished right with me, and we alternated every lure of the ton I had brought along and went through his huge tackle box four times. For a solid week, from dawn until dusk, we didn't get a nibble.

As far as I'm concerned, Puddin' Head is the sorriest bass guide in

California—and possibly in the Western Hemisphere. If there were any doubts about this, he dispelled them a week after I left when one of his customers caught a 15-pound largemouth. If Puddin' Head had been a half-way decent guide, he'd have put *me* onto that bass!

Reach Out and Punch Someone

There are times when I wonder if the telephone is really necessary. Perhaps you've felt the same way?

Last fall I was jangled out of bed at 2 a.m. on Sunday by a persistent ringing that refused to go away. I finally lifted the phone from the hook, dreading to learn what emergency had struck.

There were three hysterical voices jabbering on the other end of the wire and in the background there seemed to be a rinky-dink piano. At the same moment, my two dogs decided to exercise the cat and she treed on top of my head.

After 10 or 15 minutes, I still did not know who was calling or why. I finally shouted, "If you will nominate a spokesman, maybe I can find out what is going on."

There was a sudden hush and then a guttural voice rushed in. Although I had not heard it for four years, I knew it was John Doe, Arapahoe Indian helper for Catch Bodiford, my favorite hunting guide out in Washakie County, Wyoming.

John Doe was excited and speaking in Arapahoe. I screamed, "For God's sake, you know I don't understand Arapahoe!"

The gutteral voice changed to a different guttural. John Doe had switched over to Shoshone or Cheyenne. I whistled shrilly into the phone, there was a pause, and I could hear the confusion of an excited discussion.

Another voice came on. "Charley, old buddy, buddy, I'm calling you from Ten Killer, Wyoming, to tell you that you're the greatest guy who ever lived. You're the dearest, kindest, noblest man I ever knew."

I cut in, "Who the hell are you?"

"Why, Charley, this is C. Walter Manville from your home state and you're the dearest friend I ever had. Charley, I want you to get on a plane and come right out here. We'll meet you in Casper or Denver or wherever."

My mind was racing. Who was Walter Manville? I didn't know anybody named Manville.

Then Catch Bodiford was on the line, with just a trace of Virginia accent and a hint of an Indiana twang. "Charley, I want to thank you for sending Walt out here. He done shot the biggest muley between the Wind River and the South Fork of the Powder."

Then I remembered Walt Manville. I'd met him exactly one time, crossing trails with him while out hunting chucks in the hilly pasture country. He'd asked me where he could go to shoot a big mule deer and I naturally told him to contact Catch Bodiford.

Walt came on the line again. The full trauma of taking a record muley was upon him. He told me the whole story of how he shot the buck. Or, at least he would have if he had not broken down in tears. I am reluctant to say that Walt was totally hysterical but he did call me "mother" several times.

After Walt collapsed to the floor, John Doe got the phone and said he wanted to sing me an Arapahoe chant to the fallen buck. He paused a moment and asked me to wait until he turned off the piano player. I heard something which sounded like a hurled beer bottle ricocheting down a keyboard and then John Doe started his lament.

I was glad when Catch took the phone. John's lousy at Indian singing, even if he can do a great imitation of Elvis Presley. Catch said, "Charley, you get right on the next plane. You ain't ever seen such a rack in your life. They's tines, buttons, branches, forks, spikes, and bow ties. That old muley would embarrass a bull elk or moose to death. When you coming out, Charley?"

"Catch, ain't a 2,500-mile round trip a little far just to see a dead deer?"

He snapped back, "Not for this here deer it ain't! This deer's something special."

"What you boys drinking?" I asked, trying to change the subject.

"Tea! That's by God what we're drinking. Tea! We're having a Boston Tea Party to the biggest mule deer in the whole state of Wyoming and to good old Charley who caused it all."

Then Catch told me how he knew the buck was in the area, that he'd seen the tracks the year before. He cried a little when he said he'd made a mighty vow to find that buck and slay him if it took 10 years. In all his life, he'd never seen such a buck. Now that Walt had shot him, Catch could die peacefully. There were no more worlds left to conquer.

Catch gave a long convulsive sigh. I could almost smell the fumes and wondered why they hadn't burned out the telephone wire. There was a loud crumpling noise, like a chair collapsing, and a dull thud. I guess Catch was emotionally exhausted. Anyway, Walt came on to say that Catch didn't hurt his head when he hit the floor.

Walt said they were going to hold a wake for the mule deer and he was going to wail for him in Arapahoe. I switched him off that but not from telling me six times how he shot the buck. Then John Doe took over and explained how he had tracked the monster. It sounded like they were holding Catch up when he muttered through the whole story twice. I hung up at 4 a.m. when all three were talking at the same time. I don't think they noticed.

Now, you may think this was the end of the matter. If so, you've never known someone who shot a record buck. The next night the trio phoned at midnight. The message was a little garbled but I gathered they were south of Muddy Gap and on their way to Cheyenne to show the deer head to the Governor. They told me exactly 14 times how they had taken the trophy. We all professed our undying admiration and love for one another.

In only one respect were their calls different from many others I've received over the years. Theirs weren't collect!

Divine Intervention

There is a lot of wishful thinking connected with fishing. If all the weathermen in the state predict solid rain for Saturday, it doesn't keep the angler from going fishing on that day. At least he tries to drive through the torrent to reach his favorite lake or stream. He hopes the rain will stop. Sure enough it does—on Monday night!

When an angler has planned a day of fishing, nothing will keep him from going. Neither hail, earthquake, nor hurricane will stop him. His wishful thinking is at work. Conditions will improve by the time he reaches the river, which is a lot closer because of flooding.

I have often gone beyond wishful thinking and called on divine intervention for an improvement in the weather. I am not sure about the propriety of this, and I certainly don't wish to do anything sacrilegious. It is a grey area, and sometimes I have a twinge of conscience for being selfish enough to ask for favorable weather.

There are a lot of ways of looking at requests, though. They are simple suggestions, reminders that the powers above have options and this might be a good time to use them. My beseeching is not a formal prayer but a gentle hint.

There has to be a certain amount of weather each year, and there must be some every day. Why is it so often warm on the opening of the hunting season and so windy and cold on the first fishing trip?

Those northwest cold fronts are needed early in the fall, at least to knock down the dense cover and send the bugs into hiding. The cold fronts are no longer necessary when fishing time rolls around, but one or two are always held back to make your trips memorable occasions.

It wouldn't be right to pray that a different weather system be set up. I wouldn't dare go any further than respectfully suggesting that a slight rearrangement might be considered. That is, the fair and moderate weather would come during the fishing season and the cooler weather with the start of hunting.

Whatever the propriety of the matter, I have heard many sportsmen evoke divine intervention. A typical case is when a balky motor refuses to start after your boat has been stranded for an hour or so. Wading trout fishermen, who suddenly disappear in a hole, often arise spluttering messages to any available god of fishing, I have heard divine providence appealed to when a hunter's pointer forgot his breeding and manners and chased a deer.

I suspect that sportsmen are like the ancient Greeks and Romans and have a lot of gods to call upon. There are times when every hunter or fisherman needs sympathy and understanding. A case in point is when he gets the biggest fish of his life almost to the net and the fish gives one last leap and throws the hook.

For this unhappy angler, his companion is not adequate to salve his wounds. He needs to call on the mythological god of fishing to bear witness to the injustice of it all. He made no mistake. He hooked the monster fairly, fought it with skill and, with victory only inches away, a cruel fate intervened to rob him of his triumph.

Imploring to mythological gods gets complicated. While the angler who lost the fish was fighting it and praying for success, his companion might have been praying that the fish would break free. He might not want to listen to the story of the fishing victory for the next decade, or to see the mounted fish everytime he went to his friend's home.

Also, he might not wish his friend to develop too much pride and damage his character by boasting in public. There could be a loss of humility. The angler who lost the fish might not be mature enough to cope with sudden success and local fame.

Things usually work out for the best. That is, if you are not the angler who lost the fish.

There is a great lesson to be learned from fishing. We must accept what life brings us each day. I admit, however, I've never seen anything wrong with getting all the odds one can on his side. For instance, not long ago I was forced to ride in a commercial plane, and I watched to see if any men of the cloth or nuns were going aboard. I like to sit as close to them as possible—just in case.

On this particular flight, a priest was a passenger, and I rushed to get the seat next to him. He was a big handsome fellow in a jovial mood and was on holiday for a week of fishing. He introduced himself, and it turned out that he was going to my hometown. When I told him that I also sometimes wet a line, he was delighted and launched into a comparison of bamboo, glass, graphite, and other rods.

As the plane reached the end of the taxi strip and turned to go on the main runway for takeoff, I interrupted the padre and suggested that if he was going to send any messages up, now was a good time. He smiled gently and said, "Fear not. Accept what is to be. Now, as I was saying about bamboo rods. . . ."

I had left my car at the airport, so when we landed I offered to give the father a ride into town. As we waited for our luggage to appear on the circular belt, he told me again how much he loved to fish with his bamboo rods and how he was looking forward to his outing. I suddenly saw his tubular rod case approaching on the conveyor. It was bent into a tight U shape.

The father was well trained and did not outwardly lose his composure. He barely said a word as he filled out the forms so he could be repaid for his splintered rods, but his face was a watermelon red. As we silently drove toward town, I noticed his face becoming pale. I pulled off on the shoulder near a clump of pines and asked him if he wanted to vent his feelings.

He instantly ran into the pines, shouting and wildly waving his arms as he vanished in the shadows. I could hear the rumble but could not distinguish the words. Perhaps he reverted to Gaelic. When he came back, he looked a lot better but every pine needle in that woods had wilted and turned brown.

Avoidance Techniques

A hunter basically doesn't ask a lot. Most of us just like to get away a few weekends with the boys, do some greasy cooking, quit shaving, and leave off neckties. We enjoy telling a few stories and maybe taking a little game home for the freezer. The last thing a hunter wants is problems. One reason he leaves home is to get away from problems.

It seems as if something is always causing trouble, though. The latest is the planting of marijuana on public lands. When harvested at the right time, it brings a fabulous price on the street, especially if the supply is tight in South America.

The marijuana planter likes public lands such as those owned by the national forests and the Bureau of Land Management, which also are some of the best lands open to hunting. The planter sneaks in, plants a supply in a hidden spot, works it, and then hauls it out for distribution. If the revenuers find the pot while it's growing, they don't know who it belongs to.

The illicit crop has soared beyond $8 billion in America, according to an Associated Press story. Roughly $2 billion a year of that is now from marijuana grown on the 191 million acres of national forest lands. The planters are just getting started, though. Some high-grade stuff destroyed in Florida was worth about $2,000 a plant. That kind of money could make a lot of people forget frog gigging or muskrat trapping.

Now, it may sound a little farfetched, but the next step of the pot planter is to put on hunting gear, or outdoor clothes of some kind, and go back and forth to his marijuana caches that way. Some of the baggy canvas hunting britches I've seen would hold a bale or two of pot in the seat.

What could happen is that some of the law enforcement people will try to keep everyone off of the public lands, including hunters, to try and lower the annual pot production.

The country went through a similar problem during Prohibition in the 1920's and early 1930's. It hung on in a lot of dry states up until recent years, and once in a while today a whiskey still shows up in the middle of a good deer or squirrel woods. If you ever hunted around Wilkesboro, North Carolina, or Cosby, Tennessee, you know that there were more stills than small and big game combined. Wilkesboro lead the nation in illegal white lightning and Cosby was second. In fact, it wasn't a good idea to hunt those areas if you were going to get off the road.

The owners of the stills weren't mean. They just wanted you to go somewhere else. If they happened to know you, they might ask you to stop by for some of the clear drippings. That's the last thing I ever wanted to do. If the still got raided later, I didn't want them wondering if I had revealed its hiding place.

Many a time in the Appalachian Mountains, I'd been easing along a path looking for a squirrel when I suddenly felt a circle or two of cold steel jammed into my back. I knew right off it was no squirrel. I stopped and waited for instructions. Most of the time, they were kind words, such as, "Boy, you'd git a lot more game on t'other side of that mountain."

I always immediately obeyed the instructions. I also learned not to look back. I didn't want to know the face of the man who had rammed that double-barreled shotgun into my back. I didn't figure we had much in common and under the best of circumstances probably never would get to be friends.

I had read something in fifth-grade economics about laissez-faire doctrines. The gist of it was to let things alone, and it sure seemed to apply to any territory where mash was bubbling or the coil was dripping 140 proof.

I've run into a lot of still guards in the swamps. It seems to me that their favorite gun was the old Winchester Model 94. It was short, light, carried a lot of cartridges, and handled fast in the brush. You never knew how long a guard might have been watching you. He probably had you figured out as a hunter rather than a revenuer a long time before you saw him.

It probably got dull on the trail and they craved a little excitement. They'd hide behind a big tree by a path and let you pass. Then they'd ram that 30/30 into your back. Or maybe just lever the action. It didn't make much difference. Either way they'd paralyze you.

Some of them liked to talk for a spell. They'd want to know if I'd seen any other vehicles where I parked or anyone else in the woods. Others would just take their rifle barrels, point them, and never say a word. The direction they pointed was the direction you walked for 45 minutes or so before you went back to hunting.

Because I either hunted or fished in the woods just about the year-round, I got to know a lot of white-lightning makers by sight, which was as well as I wanted to know them. I also figured out that I never wanted to be seen with any lawmen around town, especially the revenuers. If somebody's still got busted, I didn't want the moonshiners to think I had carried any messages.

Well, the stills are about gone. I haven't run into a big one in several years. Once in a while I find an old spot that used to house a dandy, but only junk, brass, zinc, and charred wood are left.

Now with this pot coming along, I'm wondering if hunters are going to have to go through a similar thing. Every time they see a suspicious opening in the forests or BLM lands, are they going to have to make a detour?

I just hope the game doesn't take a liking for those scattered plots of marijuana. There's no telling what a buck in rut might do if he got to eating those plants. Some game may have already started chewing it. Last season, I had five coveys of quail fly straight at me and one bird on point rared up and spit in my setter's eye!

Bearing with Bruins

If there's one thing tourists like to see in the wilderness, it's bears. The bears don't necessarily feel the same way.

A good distance for seeing a bear is three miles, down hill. When the bear meanders northward, you head south.

An experienced woodsman does not like to socialize with bears too intimately. Tourists and other parttime outdoorsmen like to get as close to bears as they can for taking photographs.

According to the National Wildlife Federation, bear behavior in national parks is changing because the animals learn to associate people with free food. With the black bear, which seldom weighs more than 300 or 400 pounds, the designs are usually on the food tourists are toting. If you donate the food in a hurry, the bear usually will forget about you.

Sometimes the bears get upset because you aren't toting any food or not as much as the bear thinks you ought to have. The bears basically don't trust you and may want to put you on the ground so that you can be conveniently searched.

Once, while trout fishing a national park, I felt the fish in my creel bumping around. In fact, they were jumping more violently than their length and weight justified. I slapped at the nylon creel trailing from my left hip and felt a wet nose. The nose belonged to a gaunt sow bear.

I have always prided myself on the instant decision I made—that skinny bear needed my four trout worse than I did. In fact, I wanted her to have them—quickly! She didn't look like a patient bear who would figure out the location to the opening of the creel. I would have given her creel and all, but the creel was attached to my fishing vest, and I was wrapped inside the vest like a sausage in a bun.

I was glad to make an offering to the bear. One should always be eager to provide for wildlife. As fast as I could pull out the trout. I tossed them at the old sow, and she caught them like a trained seal.

When the fourth and last of the trout was tossed, I knew I had a problem. The old bear still looked hungry. I made another instant decision. I decided that she could fish the creek we were on, and I would fish one across the next four ridges.

She may only have been a garbage-can bear used to begging from sightseers and scrounging from garbage dumps, but I didn't know that much about her disposition. I did notice that her claws and teeth were as long as a nongarbage bear's. She had the basic equipment to disrupt anyone's trout fishing.

Grizzly bears are a worse problem. A big one may be 10 feet tall and weigh up to 1,500 pounds. Grizzlies like to blackmail tourists for food. If a hiker is shy of food, then the hiker himself may be considered a reasonable substitute.

In the United States, the grizzly is a threatened species and is seldom encountered except in national parks. That's where all the people collect. This creates a conflict of interest. Americans want to have a few grizzlies in remote areas. On the other hand, hikers and campers insist on looking at them and invading the bear's territory.

In Montana's Glacier National Park, 21 people have been injured and three killed by grizzlies since 1956. Park officials report that some of the attacks were without provocation. That's a silly statement. If a fisherman invades a grizzly's territory, that's provocation enough. When you're 10 feet tall and weigh 1,500 pounds, you can provoke anything you want.

Park authorities report that one woman had to take refuge in a back-country outhouse while a bear stood outside scratching at the walls all night. Well, if you have to be that close to a bear, I can't think of a more appropriate place to be. Of course, the woman might have misunderstood the motives of the grizzly. Maybe it just wanted to use the outhouse.

The federation has a list of things to do if you meet a grizzly on a trail, and I suppose it also applies to black bears. First of all, you shouldn't panic. That's fine, but the federation doesn't tell you how *not* to panic.

"If the bear doesn't charge you, speak to it in firm, even tones and back away." Personally, I'd like more instructions than that! What specifically does one say to a 1,500 pound grizzly or a 400-pound blackie? I would certainly start off by calling him "Mister."

"Never run. Climb into a tree if possible." Again, the instructions seem incomplete. Why isn't it permissible to *run* up a tall tree?

"If the grizzly charges, shout (don't scream) at it." I wonder how a few squeaky promises might work.

"If you are attacked, try to lie face down on the ground, or curl up with your hands clasped behind your neck. Play dead. Don't struggle or cry out."

That sounds like an unrealistic set of instructions to me, a set written by someone in Washington, D.C., who has never seen a bear. I could have written the complete instructions in two words—"faint quickly!"

"If you are lucky," the federation says, "you will convince the grizzly you're not a threat."

Why not tell the bear that while you're shouting at it? And, what's wrong with waving a white handkerchief?

A Matter of Timing

Most people don't think of Florida as a good duck hunting state. Yet it winters a large variety and number of birds, as well as growing its own crop of wood ducks. The season is set late so that the largest number of ducks will be in the state for hunting.

The arrival time depends on the weather up North. This creates an ethical problem. The best thing that can happen for the Cracker duck hunter is an early blizzard in the North to drive the birds southward. But a hunter can't in good conscience pray for severe weather that causes suffering to his fellow man.

My Florida hunting companion, Odom Overfield, is a God fearing Baptist and has nothing but good will for everybody. Next to singing old-time gospel in his church choir, he likes to hunt ducks best. He gets itchy when the first flight of teal passes through in September and can hardly stand it until the main season opens in late November.

Odie sort of hedges his bets when he gets to hoping the ducks will migrate early. He told me about it while we were sitting in a blind sipping black coffee between flights and watching the decoys bobble.

"It ain't right," Odie said, "to pray that the North gets hit with a hard bunch of snow and cold. Yankees are people, too. But I don't see nothing wrong with praying that if they got to have a blizzard, it comes early. It not only pushes the ducks down, but all of those Snow Birds." (A Snow Bird is a Yankee who winters in Florida and spends a lot of money.)

Not being an authority on matters of religious communication, I had to think about Odie's logic and finally decided to say nothing. He mistook my silence for disapproval and began to defend himself.

"You know as well as I do that the North is going to get hit with some bad weather," Odie stated. "All I'm saying is that it might as well happen in November as February. I wouldn't dream of praying that the North get any *extra* blizzards. But whatever they're due to get, well, I don't see nothing wrong with praying that they get it early, but not during any holidays."

Odie's rationalizations were getting beyond me, and I was glad to see a flock of six pintails turning toward our decoys. Florida is on the 100-point system and pintails count only 10 points. The sprig is a prized bird under any system, but when you can legally take 10 of them, they're doubly welcome.

Florida duck hunting is full of surprises. One doesn't normally expect to encounter hordes of mosquitoes while sitting in a winter blind. On warm days, they come out in droves to fatten on your juices before the next cold wave hits. If you have forgotten to take bug spray, the blind sounds like distant machine-gun fire as you slap at mosquitoes. You may not believe this, but I've seen a flight of starving mosquitoes swarm over a can of bug spray, pick it up, fly off with it, and drop it outside the blind.

Odie, the same as a lot of Crackers, is immune to mosquitoes. They simply don't bite him or even try to. Odie says that if I went to church more often the mosquitoes would leave me alone, too.

I've been meaning to ask him if that also applies to cottonmouth moccasins. For certain types of hunting in warm weather, such as wood ducks in the swamps, you can get your equilibrium thrown out of gear when a big stick you step on moves. The main danger is that you might jump so high that you'd get hurt from the free fall.

When floating creeks and rivers for ducks on sunny days, you want to be careful about going under the overhanging trees. A water snake may drop out to hitch a free ride. There are a lot of harmless snakes that resemble moccasins, but all duck hunters are not good at instant identification. Every season there are several johnboats that get their bottoms shot out.

The worst a duck hunter can suffer in Florida is from the cold, especially in northern Florida. Hunters and winter fishermen think that once they pass the Florida border they are in a land of sunshine and bikinis. But the northern third of the state, and sometimes nearly all of it, gets hit with three or four arctic fronts a year. The fronts blast in with freezing winds that penetrate like a dentist's drill. I keep telling Odie it's the Northerners sending the cold fronts down to take revenge for him praying that they get early blizzards.

The best thing about the cold fronts is that they usually pass through in three or four days. Then you may be hunting ducks in your shirt sleeves. It was that kind of day this past January when I stood up in the blind to take my first shot. Just as I pulled the trigger and saw the slow flier collapse, I realized I'd shot a fulvous tree duck. It's a 100-point duck and therefore I was finished for the day.

Then I saw a long, black shape swimming toward the bird. Odie grabbed a big stick and went splashing into the hip-deep water. The seven-foot alligator barely beat Odie to the bird, time enough to open his jaws and close them around the duck, with only one foot dangling out. Odie grabbed the foot and started beating the alligator with the stick. For a few seconds, there was so much spray from tail lashing and stick pounding that I couldn't tell who was winning.

Then Odie broke free and proudly held my bird high so that I could see he'd won. As he waded back to the blind, he shouted, "No dad-gummed 'gator is going to get our ducks!"

"Why didn't you let the 'gator have him?" I asked. "Then I wouldn't have any points."

"Ain't you seen that game warden squatting in the bushes over there putting them glasses on us?"

"Well," I replied, "you just violated by molesting an alligator."

Odie grinned and said, "It ain't molesting to protect what's rightfully yours."

It was a long day as I sat there with an empty shotgun watching Odie collect 10 pintails. He said it proved I ought to go to church more often.

A Nostalgic Whiff

Science has been unable to define just how keen a human can scent. One reason is that the scenting ability of people varies. Some humans cloud their olfactory receptors with tobacco smoke, various sprays, auto emissions, garlic essence, and aftershave lotion that is guaranteed to attract hordes of females, all of whom are wearing different perfumes.

With all the scent signals the brain receives, it must think the nose has all its wires crossed. There are not only conflicting signals, but also meshed, interwoven, and unbelievable signals constantly being relayed by the nose to the brain. The brain is then supposed to make some sort of sense of the signals and interpret them for action or nonaction.

The other day a chemist asked me how far I thought I could smell different odors. Well, I'm writing this in August and I'm not having any trouble scenting the hunting season just ahead. In fact, I've been getting definite whiffs of the fall season since last spring.

I told the chemist that I planned to hunt sage grouse in Idaho. I could already smell the sagebrush, plus a grouse being cleaned after eating sage. He laughed and said he'd like to examine my nose and asked would I will it to him after my death. It was some trick, he said, to smell sage when the nearest bush was several hundred miles away.

I told him I could also smell cottonwood trees at hundreds of miles provided the leaves had turned yellow. He seemed surprised, one reason being that he thought cottonwoods didn't give off much scent, and he wanted to know what leaf color had to do with it. Of course a cottonwood tree has a distinctive odor if we stop and put our noses close to the bark and smell. If you know what one cottonwood smells like, you can assume the others smell similar. When you see a grove of cottonwoods in a dry valley from a mountaintop, you know what they smell like—a grove of cottonwoods.

It is only natural that I associate cottonwood odor with yellow leaves. I don't live in cottonwood country and the only time I see them is during the hunting season when the leaves are yellow.

Once the nose associates a particular odor with an object and the brain records it on tape, it is a record as long as the brain lives. Like an unknown book in a basement library, the scent record may lie dormant for years. If that scent is encountered again years later, though, even in the dark of a rainy night, the player turns on and the tape tells you what the scent is.

If you have ever stepped too close to a rattlesnake and heard it buzz, no matter how high you leap in a state of panic, your brain will record that particular sound. You may not hear that buzz again for 20 years, but when you do you will instantly recognize it, and probably leap again.

Likewise, when a rattler is shedding its skin, the lubricant for loosening the skin has a definite odor. Once you've imprinted that scent on your brain's tape, you will recognize it instantly when you cross it again.

A wet whitetail leaves an odor in the brush, and a rutting buck leaves a distinctive odor in cool, humid weather. Wild boars or feral hogs leave a definite odor under certain conditions that are favorable to the human receptors.

The classic wildlife-scent dispenser is the skunk. Even a city nose, defiled and burned out with assorted foreign substances, can instantly detect essence of angry skunk. It will be recorded in your brain's index file. Five years later, if you see a happy skunk at 100 yards that is not squirting, the obnoxious odor may come back, or seem to come back.

During the hunting season, it's important to store information on your memory tape so that you can play back the desirable parts in the off-season. The visual parts of the tape are perhaps the easiest to turn on, but many sounds can be easily recalled. For instance, if you've ever been someplace you shouldn't have been in the dark of night, and suddenly heard a rifle bolt slammed shut, it darn sure registers "10 by 10" and is forever recallable.

In those golden moments of reverie when you're replaying an old hunting trip in your mind as you recline in your easy chair, the movie will be more complete and fulfilling if you dub in the smells along with the sights, sounds, and other senses. It is easy to remember the sight of a pan of frying bacon, the sounds of sizzling and popping grease, and maybe the pangs of hunger in your anxious stomach. It takes a little practice to reach deeper and fetch the pleasant smells. It can be done, though. It's in your computer. A lot depends on how well you can relax and how smoothly you let your computer work.

The odors drifting from the first pot of morning coffee are so pleasant and sensuous that they are easy to recall, sometimes even by brand. Flapjacks vary, depending on composition and other factors. Experienced sourdough cooks can take a whiff and tell you how long the dough has been nursed. Cathead biscuits, whether made with buttermilk or branch water, have a fresh, distinctive smell.

Fried country ham for breakfast has a much different odor than sausage, the latter varying greatly by the amount of spices used by the blender. The basic sausage smell is always there, though. A thick bulldog gravy's odor is not remotely like redeye gravy's. When one is recalling past camp breakfasts, there's no way the two could be confused.

When I relax in an easy chair and think of past hunting trips, I like to smell the stews. To a city dweller, they might all look and smell much alike. Stews vary with the cooks, however. They also are distinctive in odor, each cook using his own favorite seasonings.

I've been eating the stews of Elias Hornby for 20 years or more at various camps. No two ever tasted exactly the same. He couldn't write you a recipe for his stews if he tried. He uses a pinch of this, a dab of that, and a shake of something else. He's an artist. Each stew is a creative adventure that he has no interest in duplicating. His artistic stamp is on each batch, and I'd recognize the odor of one if I was blindfolded in the middle of Siberia. I can't dream about the camps we've been to or think about Hornby's black stew kettle without the delightful smells returning.

You easily remember, of course, the glory times, such as when you take a big antelope or shoot your first elk or get a double on woodcock. The amount of time we spend pulling the trigger on any hunting trip is mighty small. For the long haul, it's the routine things we do that use most of our time. Its important that we record the mental and sensory perceptions in our data file. They come in real handy during the off-season and at odd moments anytime.

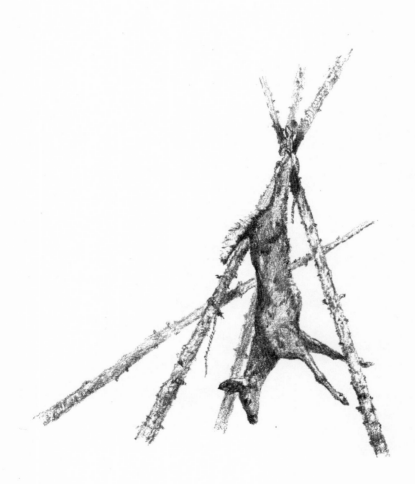

All the Comforts of Deer Camp

There are a lot of reasons that deer camps should be kept neat and clean. There is not only the sanitary aspect but the morale factor. The British Army long ago found that its troops did better, even when living in muddy trenches, if each soldier shaved every day.

Another reason for policing the camp is that if you don't move out some of the old junk, you won't have room for new junk.

Yet another reason for cleaning camp is that you may have visitors, and you want the place to look reasonably neat. A plush club of oil men from New Orleans and Baton Rouge had another reason for a big field day at their lodge in western Alabama, according to a story currently making the rounds. They employed a local maid and cook to get the camp in shape and stocked the icebox with gourmet food.

One weekend, four of the members came to the camp and each brought a guest. The "guests" were from the chorus line of a prominent nightclub in New Orleans. Although "guests" of this nature were not completely unheard of in the camp, seldom did they stay longer than one evening. Because this was a protracted holiday and the members were a bit uneasy, the young ladies were introduced to the maid and cook as wives of the four members. The members also brought along their rifles and hunting gear.

After all, they were married, and it was vital that their real wives be convinced that they were hunting.

The "wives" and the four members had visions of a truly festive weekend. They were blissfully unaware that the real wives, back in Louisiana, had gotten together and decided to drive to the lodge and surprise their husbands.

The four wives arrived dressed up in their fur coats and high heels. The maid, who happened to be sweeping the front porch, was the first one to see them. The maid, wise to the ordinary indiscretions of the camp, was protective of her generous employers. Totally convinced that the ladies in residence *were* married to the members, she yelled at the four wives, "You street gals can't come up here. These gentlemen is here with their wives, and we don't allow any funny stuff. You gotta get right outta here."

The final report on the incident is that the camp is in shambles. The chimney still stands and part of the foundation is salvageable. The perennial food patches are in good shape, but the lease is up for sale.

Most deer camps, of course, are used strictly as headquarters for hunting deer. One of the reasons for going to camp is that a man has the choice of making or not making his bed. He can leave his long handles where they fall, unless he's afraid his buddies will tie knots in the legs. He doesn't have to comb his hair, shave, or change underwear until someone complains, or he can't stand himself any longer.

There comes a time, however, when the camp must be cleaned. Sometimes it would be quicker to burn the shack down and start over.

Hunters add to the problem of clutter because they are great acquisitors of anything which adds to their personal convenience. They like to leave articles at the camp, rather than hauling them back and forth.

A party which is departing after a weekend or several days also is generous in leaving odds and ends behind for the next bunch of hunters. Some of those who depart are optimists. That is, they expect half a loaf of bread to keep from the closing of one season until the opening of the next. They leave a big box of saltine crackers with only two crackers.

Deer camps are not noted for having a full box, package, or bottle of anything. All the shelf space is used up by containers only partially full. At spring cleaning, it's not unusual to find eight or so ketchup bottles almost empty. If you poured the contents of all the bottles into one, you still wouldn't have a full bottle of ketchup.

Deer hunters are basically generous people. That's what causes the problem, though! Why would anyone leave a half-consumed can of sardines? After several months of aging, the fish add more to the atmosphere than the average hunter can appreciate.

There is a limit beyond which salad dressings will keep, especially when the camp rules are to turn off the electricity after the last hunt of the season. Have you ever opened the door of a refrigerator and looked at a dozen half-filled bottles of salad dressing turned to blue mold?

Olives are another item frequently left at camp, usually with just one olive in about four inches of juice. Deer hunters must eat a lot of pizza; otherwise, why would there be so many old olive bottles standing around?

Do you know what is the dirtiest thing in camp at spring cleanup? If you don't, you've been avoiding the spring detail. It's the soap bottles and boxes, that's what! There are at least 35 partly filled bottles of detergent, and everyone with dirty, greasy, or bloody hands has handled them. The sink and dishes finally may have gotten their just due, but the detergent bottles are black with grime.

Every hunter who comes to camp brings a bottle of detergent and then prays that someone else will use it. What no one ever remembers to bring is a bar of bath soap. Have you ever tried to take a shower at a camp lucky enough to have such an installation? If so, you've never found a piece of soap larger than a dime.

There may be several of these lying on the shower floor or trying to escape down the drain. The fragments are contorted and twisted where past showerees have tried to squeeze out enough lather to wash behind their ears. If you're desperate enough, you may find a chip outside the shower which the others have overlooked. It takes a lot of soap to get the scent masker and essence of doe urine off your hide, but there usually isn't enough soap to soak the subsoil out of one fingernail. If you're desperate enough, of course, you can make a mad dash to the kitchen sink and grab an old bottle of detergent. Even so, no one ever washes off the outside of the detergent bottle.

Of all the excess material which accumulates at deer camp, bath towels are not among it. No one ever remembers to bring a towel, not even the meticulous hunter who keeps a checkoff list. He may bring a full set of reloading equipment so that he can adjust his cartridges for wind, humidity, and excessive gravitational pull from a full moon. He brings all sorts of powder cans, bullets, and primers but never a bath towel.

In any deer camp in the New World, there is one house towel. It is of an indeterminate age, some place between early Pilgrim and last season. Since its first wetting, it has never seen sunlight. It hangs stiffly from a 40-penny nail just outside the shower. Whether the camp has four members or 40, the towel impartially serves all who forgot to bring a fresh towel, which is just about everybody.

No one ever mentions the towel, or thinks of replacing it. No one ever hangs it in the sun. Each member uses it after taking a shower and hangs it back in the same place. A member may balk at using it, realizing that it has massaged countless bodies, but he has no alternative. To benefit himself of what sanitation is available, he dries himself with the outside edges. He figures that immediate past-users patted down with the middle of the towel . . . they didn't. They all used the edges. In fact, the center of the towel is virgin territory.

When the camp towel finally crumples and falls to rags, someone will replace it. No one will ever know who did, though.

The members of every deer club know they will track through swamp muck, red clay, peat, or some combination thereof. Whatever the soil content of their lease, a good portion will be dirt which clings to their boots and lower britches. For those who wade beaver bottoms, there will be pratfalls and bellybusters. A considerable acreage of topsoil will cling to their outer garments and be brought back to camp.

Realizing this problem in advance, there is always one member who brings a coarse mat and metal boot wiper for the opening of a new club. They are placed right outside the main entrance door so that hunters can easily clean their boots before entering. No one ever uses them.

It is a curious thing about hunters, but they always think their boots are clean. It's someone else who keeps bringing in huge mud clumps or blotches of red clay. The ones who track in and deposit coarse sand are probably the worst of all. Sand is harder than steel, and when it is scattered over the lodge floor it grinds and cuts each time another hunter walks across it. It does make for unique floor patterns, once the sand and muck are washed off. In fact, there is a deer club in New York which took up part of its flooring and won first place in a modern art show in the city. The critics raved about the unique brush strokes.

One reason the mats and scrapers are not used at the main entrance is that each member prefers to enter by the kitchen. This does nothing for the cook's disposition and often results in a change of camp cooks. This stops no one from entering through the kitchen, however.

For rainy days at camp, hunters are good about bringing old outdoor magazines and leaving them. When you want to read a magazine, there are only pieces around. There never seem to be many good fire-starters around camp, and parts of magazines are used to keep a dying flame fluttering for a while. It never pays to start reading a story unless you're sure no pages are missing. Just when it gets to the part about how the author was putting the sights on old Cow-Hoof, a record-book buck, the story leaps to the back of the magazine, which is missing. You lie awake all night wondering if the author hit or missed the monster buck.

Worthwhile reading is usually stored in a safe place, which is what you would expect for good literature. It's surprising at spring cleaning time how many copies of *Penthouse*, *Playboy*, and *Ecstasy* are found under mattresses.

No one ever puts up a current calendar at camp, or takes down one that has been fading for several eons. The only way that a calendar comes down is like the community towel, for it to crumple to pieces. It may be that new calendars are hung but, if so, somebody takes them down to use as targets for sighting-in a rifle. Pages from *Penthouse* are never used for sighting rifles or patterning buckshot.

One of the most interesting items at many deer camps is the communal dining table. It has everything except a place to put your knife, fork, and plate.

Nobody ever throws anything away from the dining table. It sags under the weight of bottles without labels, whetstones, rifle-cleaning kits, hunting knives, and parts of things for which no one knows the original use. One camp is reported to have had a copy of Amy Vanderbilt's book on etiquette. This seems doubtful, because the pages would be too handy for starting fires.

The dining table always has many cartons of half-filled cracker boxes, the remnants of late-night snacks, or broken crackers the inspired creators of hors d'oeuvres wouldn't use for their masterpieces. There is never a full box of napkins, but there are usually six or eight partial boxes, plus the bare rollers from three rolls of paper towels.

There are bottles of hot, barbecue, homemade, and pepper sauces, and at least five bottles of grape jelly left from various breakfasts. The favorite condiment of each member is somewhere on the table. The trick is uncovering it. The centerpiece contains three greasy decks of cards and at least a dozen jokers from decks long since worn to a frazzle. There are two flashlights, neither of which works.

Two or three Bermuda onions give fragrance to a can of gun oil. There are toothpicks, empty cigarette packages, and a folded aerial photo of the lease, which someone tried to preserve with syrup. There is no telling what one might find if one took the time to pry beneath the clutter.

Things such as cobwebs don't bother hunters. Sometimes they get so thick and heavy you can hang a pair of hunting britches on them. Dirt-dobber nests add charm, and no one complains of wasp nests unless its residents become hostile. A certain ambience is expected of deer camps. Old antlers, moth-eaten hides, and arrowheads only make the camp rustic.

Every deer camp ought to be cleaned at least once a year. If you're on the detail, it's much like being on a treasure hunt. You never know what you'll find. One hunter found his long lost tuxedo hanging under an old poncho. He claims he has no recollection of ever wearing a tuxedo to camp. If he had worn it, the chances are unlikely that any of his buddies would have let him forget it. Still, though, the tuxedo was there.

There's a lot to be said for the hunter who owns a motor home. He drives it home after the deer season and looks so pitiful that his wife finally cleans it.

Early Training

Back in ancient times when I hunted as a boy, farmers went to town on Saturdays and church on Sundays. In between, they didn't see many people. When you stopped by their homes to ask permission to hunt, they were anxious to talk, especially if they thought you had any scandalous news from town.

It always paid to carry them a tidbit or two of gossip. If I didn't know any, I'd make up some to keep them happy. It was the least I could do in return for them letting me hunt. I wouldn't use local names where somebody might be hurt and invented names for traveling salesmen. All traveling salesmen were suspected of leading sinful lives, and it gave you a lot of leeway when hinting of lurid activities as late as 10 p.m.

There was no television then and not many farmers owned a radio. They were still debating on whether or not to put in electric lights. If a farmer had to make a telephone call, he'd drive a Model A Ford to a crossroads store, or maybe he'd hitch up a mule to get there. Telephones were only for emergencies. If someone got called to the store to return a phone call, it meant close kin had died or were about to. Telegrams were always bad news. Somebody in the family had been in an accident, or, even worse, a distant cousin urgently needed money.

If you hunted a lot, it meant you had to have a fresh supply of stories. It didn't take a kid long to figure out that farmers didn't want any bad news; they had enough of that right on their own place. They didn't expect good news either, because there wasn't any good news a youngster could bring. The farmers wanted something juicy, a spicy little tidbit they could roll around while they were following four mules and a harrow up and down endless rows.

Back in those days, it didn't take much to make a juicy story. If you got a swift glimpse of a woman's knee, it was startling enough to be worth telling. If you saw where she rolled her stocking just above the knee, a farmer was ready to hear all the details, and so were the older boys down at the pool hall. If a lady at church got careless in crossing her legs and there was a flash of white above the knee, the town talked about it for a month. After all, ladies weren't supposed to cross their legs and get comfortable in church. They were expected to sit and suffer like everybody else.

The only acceptable pornography around was the corset ads in mail-order catalogs. Newspapers didn't dare run ads of women in undergarments. A boy, or a farmer for that matter, stealing looks at painted catalog models clad in bloomers didn't dare be caught. He kept one finger in the section on guns while he sneaked a look at the bloomered, corseted models and wondered what was underneath. If anyone came near, he quickly flipped to the gun section. He couldn't run the risk of being called a sex fiend all over town.

I developed a problem with one farmer, old man Henry Rayfield. He got to waiting for me every afternoon about 45 minutes after school let out (that's how long it took to ride to his farm on my bicycle). He'd be leaning across a fence post down by his mailbox chewing on his fortieth straw of the day.

"Well," he'd say, "what's the latest news in town?"

If I hadn't picked up any choice gossip, I'd have to invent some. Lightning rod salesmen with thin, black mustaches were always good for a story, especially if they stayed at Miss Fanny's Boarding House and joked with the chubby waitresses. There were still mule traders in those days, and they came from way off and were easy to make up stories about. Widow ladies were fair game for salesmen, or drummers, as they were called back then. We didn't have any divorcees, the only ones at that time being in Hollywood.

It got to be a real problem thinking up fresh scandals, especially because I didn't dare use local names. I did the best I could, though, because old man Henry Rayfield had more rabbit fields than any farmer in the county. On top of that, he let me use his rabbit dog Beetle, which was part beagle and the rest traveling salesman. Beetle, which old man Henry thought was the way to pronounce *beagle*, could push a cottontail in a circle better than any dog I ever knew.

To keep old man Henry happy, I began going to the school library and thumbing through *National Geographic* magazines. It was okay to run pictures of naked statues as long as they were from Europe, because that was art. Because the magazine was also educational, it was all right to run pictures of topless or naked women as long as the models weren't Americans.

When no one in the library was looking, I'd cut out some of the pictures. I knew for a fact that old man Henry appreciated them more than anybody. Besides, he had as much right to be educated as anybody else. To this day, I've never seen a man who was more interested in geography than old man Henry!

The trouble was that old man Henry got to expecting wilder and wilder stories from me. My detailed knowledge was severly restricted, but I looked up some books about European royalty and converted their activities to our area.

Naturally I wasn't hunting on just one farm. Whenever I made up a story that old man Henry liked, I'd use it at other farms. Even back then I didn't have a good memory and never told a story the same way twice. How could a poor schoolboy know the farmers were comparing his stories when they met down at the general store?

I got carried away trying to please old man Henry one day and told him a hardware salesman, who stayed at Miss Fanny's every two weeks, was slipping out to visit a prominent citizen's wife. Well, old man Henry got to pressing me for details and names. There weren't any names, or course, but I got excited and blurted out the name of the wife of a town preacher. About details, I couldn't say much. As far as I knew, that preacher's wife wasn't good at checkers and I knew her religion didn't allow her to play cards. Personally, I didn't know why the imaginary hardware salesman would want to see her late at night in the first place—that is, unless he liked to sing church songs.

It turned out later that old man Henry went to church in town, the very one where that wife's husband preached. That in itself was something a poor growing boy could hardly know, it being the common practice for farmers to attend rural churches in groves of old trees with family cemetery plots in consoling distance of the preaching and singing.

Old man Henry made it a point to do some checking and he was real upset the next time I stopped by to help him with his rabbit problem. He lit into me and scared me half to death, finally making me admit I had been inventing the stories all along.

He ended up shouting, "I'm disappointed in you and I'll bet my best mule you'll never amount to a hill of beans. You'll probably end up being one of those good-for-nothing writer fellows!"

Over the years, I've thought a lot about what old man Henry said. Now, when I talk with a farmer, I stay on safe ground with topics such as how the dad-gummed government ought to do more for farmers.

Just One More Time

The place an outboard motor is most likely to conk out is where you've passed the point of no return. That means it's closer to nearly anywhere in the world than the marina where your car's parked.

Outboards are good at spluttering and dying when you've taken your boss near the end of a scenic inlet he didn't want to go to in the first place. He kept hinting that he'd be happier at the dock peeling tops off aluminum cans, but you insisted on showing him a secret area of primitive beauty.

A lot of improvements have been made to outboard motors. Now they only shudder and pass away when you're downstream from the launching ramp.

My wife basically doesn't understand the internal combustion engine, but she usually has a lot to say when my outboard gives up the ghost. Even when it's just come back from the shop, she says she's heard cigarette coughs that sound better.

I have a theory that no mechanical device is worth owning unless it can be fixed by glaring, kicking, or cussing at it. Outboard motors don't qualify in any of these categories.

They come close in the cowling department. Sometimes I can stomp and kick the cowling until it snaps back in place. The cowling is a decoration, though, a sort of skin to catch loose parts that fly off. It, unfortunately, has nothing to do with getting you back to your car.

What an outboard motor does better than anything else in the world is catch, run smoothly for three seconds, and then faint from exhaustion. There is nothing that will build your hopes so high and then crash them so cruelly, with the exception of some of the girls I knew back in high school.

If the motors would just go ahead and die, then one could give them a decent burial by commending them to the deep. If you yank the starter cord long enough, though, you can always get at least one encouraging gasp of life.

When you're 10 miles from the dock, and a rainstorm is about to hit, any little *chug-chug* or vibration is enough to build false hopes. Sometimes the motor may purr like a tabby cat with a saucer of milk. About the time you smile and let out a big "wheee," the motor coughs and dies with the finality of your line being snapped by a big bass.

Over the years, of course, one learns certain tricks of resurrection. First, I ask my companion if he knows anything about motors. If he can say as much as "duh," I turn the problem over to him. I always try to encourage him by handing him a tool kit from my tackle box. Because the tools are too large for reels, I figure they must have been designed for reluctant motors. Anyway, they came with the box when I bought it at a blind auction.

I realize there are certain first aid functions one can perform. For instance, I know to check the tank to see if it has gas. That may sound like a silly statement, but it's more than our kids ever learned with the family cars. Gas tanks, which sit up awhile can accumulate all sorts of foreign objects such as dirt-dobber nests, sand piles, and humidity, which had no other place to go.

There is also something about a certain ratio of oil to the amount of gasoline. It stays out of whack because no container of oil matches a full tank of gas. Because the oil is open anyway, it's easier just to go ahead and pour it in.

A long unmanageable gas line runs from the tank to the motor. Handling it is like trying to tie a clinch knot in a boa constrictor. The main purpose of such a long line is to have something else in the boat to trip over. Or, if your motor falls off the transom, maybe you can drag it back with the gas line.

If the line is screwed correctly into the motor and gas tank, but the motor doesn't run, the choke is in the wrong position. The choke is always in the wrong place. If it isn't, it will be before you get the motor spitting.

After you get confused with the choke, there's another gadget to test. It's a bulb on the gas line which either increases the gas pressure or pushes all the water back into the gas tank. I forget which.

There are 342 different combinations in which you can arrange the various external gadgets, a sort of geometric progressive series of Academy Awards to the marvels of science. With each arrangement, you pull the starter cord. If there is no encouraging splutter after 10 pulls of the cord, you have chosen a wrong combination and you move on to the next one. When your right arm becomes paralyzed from yanking the cord, it is all right to change to your left. If severe chest pains develop, pause for a minute and try to remember if you have written a will.

When you have exhausted the 342 combinations, wait until a kind soul comes along who will tow your boat back to the dock. Then, take your motor to a factory-certified repair shop.

When you can't get someone to wait on you, go ahead and join the coffee break. After you finally attract the attention of a kid with long hair and dirty bluejeans, plead with him to look at your motor. The first question he'll ask is, "What's the matter with it?"

Stay calm! Don't give the kid a smart answer such as, "It has the chicken pox." He might go back and join the card game.

After you struggle to get the motor unloaded from your car trunk, the kid will mount it on the edge of a 55-gallon drum filled with water. He'll click a few gadgets, give the starter cord a gentle tug, and your motor will catch and hum like a wife with a dozen roses when it isn't even her birthday.

The kid will then stare at you as if you're a complete idiot.

Purdy is as Purdey Does

A Purdey shotgun is the Rolls-Royce of all shotguns. It's a side-by-side double handcrafted in England, and a new one costs about what it takes to send a youngster to a state university for four years.

I realize there's no set figure for what it costs to send a kid to college. It depends on how high he lives. Well, it's the same with a Purdey. There's a base charge, but when you start adding frills and inlays it's a good idea to own several producing oil wells.

On top of the cost, you have to be a tycoon or at least vice-president of a fair-sized country to get delivery in less than three years. Even secondhand Purdeys increase in value each year and are in constant demand as good investments.

It is understandable why wealthy hunters like to buy Purdeys and other expensive English doubles. There's not much point in being rich if you're going to shoot the same kind of shotgun as most of us, one right off the rack

There's a certain snob appeal in Purdey shotguns. I've known a couple of hunters who sold their homes to buy matched pairs. They weren't snobbish about it. They just loved fine shotguns more than they did fine homes. It's usually their friends who are snobbish because they know somebody who owns a matched pair and have actually been afield with them.

Some owners of Purdeys never hunt with them, but hang them on their walls to show admiring friends. I used to hunt chukar in Idaho and Oregon with a friend who toted a Purdey. I could never enjoy the hunt because he treated that museum piece as if it was an old wreck he'd bought out of a hockshop. He used it as a staff to help him over rocks and up cliffs, and it had more dents than a snooker table in a funny farm. The gun was perpetually thirsty for a taste of oil and had more rust freckles than a junkyard full of 55-gallon drums rescued from saltwater. I used to feel so sorry for the Purdey that I'd sneak it out at night when we were camping and soak it in gun oil.

Some Purdey admirers buy them as works of art. They don't collect paintings and sculpture, but Purdey shotguns. One rich man I know sleeps with his. He makes his wife sleep in another bedroom down the hall. He says the shotgun is prettier than she is and has better lines. It comforts him when he awakens in the middle of the night to look at the gold inlay work. She says she would divorce him if she thought she'd be awarded the Purdey and could keep her Rolls-Royce. What she wants to do is take that shotgun and place it under a drop forge.

The main value of a custom shotgun used for shooting is that it is tailored to fit you. No matter how off-center your physical dimensions, the finished shotgun fits snugly with a proper cheek-eye-muzzle relationship, provided you mount it correctly every time. Also, you can have each barrel bored for the choke percentage you desire, such as the right barrel to pattern 44 percent and the left 79.

I have never envied the hunter who owned a Purdey. Mostly I am too old to worry about material things beyond my means. I have always wanted to own the Washington Monument, but have about given it up as an unrealistic goal. Most shotgunners, however, have a secret yearning to someday be the proud owner of a Purdey.

There has been only one time in my life when I used a Purdey to good advantage. It was an imaginary Purdey, and I handled it with the knowledge that many shotgun men nurse a secret desire to pick up a Purdey at bargain-basement prices, or less.

The morning before the deer season opened a few years ago, my boss cornered me and said he had four important customers coming in that afternoon who insisted on going deer hunting. He knew I'd be happy to take them to the Spit and Argue Buck Club to which I belonged. I tried to explain that we had only 10 members and it was an ironclad rule that nobody could bring a visitor for the opening weekend. The only exception would be if a member dropped out or dropped dead, but no one ever had—not for the opener.

My boss is a kind and understanding man. He smiled and said, "I'm sure you'll find a way, if you want to keep your job. I'll even forget that you've had eight operations to have your tonsils removed during the past nine hunting seasons."

Traditionally, the 10 members meet at 2 p.m. on Friday to get the camp cleaned and stocked with groceries and refreshments. I didn't arrive until 4 p.m., trying to think of a way to get four spaces. I had an idea, though, when I remembered that a second cousin of mine had died upstate the previous weekend and I had gone up to try to help sell off some junk hunting and fishing gear for the widow. Because they had formerly lived in our town, the club members knew them.

When I reached camp, the members kidded me about being late to avoid the cleaning detail. I apologized and told them I had just returned from Cousin Jenny's, trying to sell the gun collection she was stuck with. I casually added, "There was an old double with a straight stock, no pistol grip, that had a funny name. It was Purkey or Purdue or Putey or something like that. You fellows ever here of a shotgun by that name? I started to buy it to help Cousin Jenny, but she wanted too much money, something like $200."

Well, one by one five members called me off to the side and asked for more details on that shotgun and exact directions to Cousin Jenny's house. It seemed they were all charitable and wanted to help her immediately. I told each one, "Look, I wouldn't drive 300 miles up there and miss the opening weekend. Besides, she might have already sold all the guns."

By 5 p.m., eight of the members had found urgent reasons why they couldn't wait to help Cousin Jenny. The camp was deserted except for me and old Ross Harkins. He looked me over with a crafty smile and said, "I know you. If there was a Purdey shotgun at Jenny's for $200 or $2,000, you'd have bought it!"

I replied, "Ross, what's a Purdey?"

Anyway, I went back to town and got the boss's four guests and brought them out for a weekend of deer hunting. No one in our club bought a Purdey from Cousin Jenny that weekend, so I guess they must have gotten there too late.

A Helping Hand

If you live to be old enough, one day it will occur to you that you cannot remember what you ate for breakfast, but you vividly recall a dove shoot a half a century ago. You can remember the hunt in color or black-and-white, even how the hunters looked and what some of them said.

If you are relaxed enough for the recesses of your memory to open wide, you remember individual shots made on those long-ago mornings. As you shivered at the base of a dead walnut tree, you saw the flocks hurtling low in the dim light on their first feeding pass of a new day.

The corn, waiting to be picked by hand, was a mottled brown and the rows stood like lonely lines of soldiers. Part of the field had already been harvested, and the doves would land on the bare spots to search for the yellow kernels. When the field finally had been picked, hogs would be let in to have a harvest of their own. That's when the biggest dove shoot of the season would be held, with some of the gunners driving out in their Model T's from farm towns as far away as 20 miles.

It was a good time for a farm kid to make some money, especially if his dad had a tractor. Some of the Model T's always got stuck on the muddy roads and the town dudes would pay a lot, sometimes as much as a dollar, to be pulled out. If your farm didn't have a tractor, you could pull the cars out of the muck with a team of mules. You just couldn't cover as many of the country roads with a team as you could with a tractor.

The boys under 10 served as pickup boys, general errand runners and, if they were responsible enough, gun bearers. You did whatever was necessary to help your gunner save his energy for pulling the trigger. It was the standard training every boy went through while he was slowly growing old and large enough to be one of the shooters.

If the gunner you were assigned to did a good job of shooting, he might tip you. All of us tried to get city sports because they were more likely to tip than the community shooters. Tips were your best way to get money for Christmas and might be your only chance at real cash. In our community everybody did favors for everybody else. There wasn't much cash to change hands.

The city of Greenville was said to have almost 8,000 people and was the largest place most of us had ever been to. The Greenville gunners were the biggest tippers and the ones the pickup boys tried to get. Aside from the tip, however, we would have picked up the doves free. The shoots were the biggest social doings of the year, unless there was a murder trial at the county seat. All the ladies got together and cooked enough food for noon dinner to break down a couple of tables. Sometimes there was a famous stump speaker, a politician trying to get reelected to office. He'd talk for an hour after dinner, promising the farmers what he was going to do for them. They knew he'd never get anything done, but they'd vote for him anyway, especially if he was a good shot.

Shells were expensive back in those days, costing as much as 75 cents a box. The hunters who could afford it took a full case to their stands. Those who couldn't took the odds and ends of loads they could scrape up. There weren't any dove regulations to speak of.

A case of shells came in a wooden box. It was too heavy for a small boy to tote in one trip. If your gunner helped you carry it, you knew he was a pretty good fellow and you'd work twice as hard spotting doves for him and picking up the ones he knocked down.

A lot of the city sports weren't used to being on their feet for long stretches, so we took small benches or upright chairs to the blinds for them. We made temporary blinds out of corn stalks and baling wire. If you drew a banker as a gunner, you always tried to get him a big chair. The bankers were usually pale, potbellied, and had eye trouble. There were a lot of things a pickup boy could do to help a banker. Because all the local farmers owed the banks, the bankers got the best stands near a dead tree or right under a main flight line. The pickup boys were given instructions to be polite, not to lose any birds, and to say "Sir" a lot.

I used to rig it so that I would get T. Phares Quillman, the Greenville banker. That suited everybody else because he seldom shot a good score. T.

Phares was talked about a lot because he wasted money shooting clay targets. I thought he was a fine fellow and had my life savings of $3.20 in his bank. Anybody generous enough to pay four percent interest just had to be a good person at heart.

I finally figured out that T. Phares couldn't shoot a good score because of his eyesight. He could not distinguish a dove once it got below the tree line and blended in with the background. I suggested he quit shooting at the low doves and take only the high ones silhouetted against the sky.

T. Phares shot a Model-12 pump with a full choke, and when he stroked that forearm it worked like a sewing machine. He could forevermore pop those doves against the blue. If he clearly saw the bird, it was a goner.

I never will forget the morning T. Phares Quillman was high gunner, with no telling how many triples. He told everybody I was the best pickup boy he'd ever seen. He even promised to help pay my way through college.

Well, that seemed like a long way off, and I had heard enough of that kind of promise from the stump speakers. With a lot of "Sirs," I did suggest that he might let me take a few shots on the next hunt. And, by golly, he did!

Dial an Excuse

A friend of mine plans to start a national telephone service for fishermen. When they run out of excuses, they phone "Dial an Excuse" and get a new one.

I'm a bit leary of investing in his idea. Most of the anglers I know are good at inventing reasons why the fish aren't hitting or why they didn't catch any when the fish did bite.

Only recently, a fisherman in the front of my boat lost a big bass that was trying to steal his plug. Before I could offer a word of condolence, he said, "I'd have landed that fish if it hadn't been for the political situation in El Salvador."

If that seems a little vague, the week before, a friend told me he missed a series of strikes because of the "Doppler Effect." I told him I wasn't sure what that was. In fact, I had never heard of it.

Here's what he said, and I made him repeat it so that I could write it down: "A Doppler Effect is an apparent change in the frequency of waves, as in sound or light, occuring when the source and observer are in motion relative to one another, the frequency increasing when the source and observer approach one another and decreasing when they move apart."

Well, with all of that going on, you can see why anybody's timing would be off on a topwater strike. You also can see why my friend was either desperate or inventive to memorize that definition. He's the kind who would go to any length to come up with a new excuse but would hardly pay to phone "Dial an Excuse."

When I returned home after the trip, I dug out a notebook from the topwater season a year ago. That was when he had used his magnetic susceptibility theory for missing strikes. I had a note that this was "the ratio of the magnetic permeability of a medium to that of a vacuum, minus one. It is positive for a paramagnetic or ferromagnetic medium and negative for a diamagnetic medium." He must read some strange outdoor magazines!

I suggested that he was giving excuses not pertaining to bass fishing. He said I was dead wrong. While his reasons might sound like something from a physics laboratory, there are all sorts of weird currents that follow fishermen. He said it was worse than ESP, and science hadn't even scratched the surface with explanations.

He said all sorts of cosmic forces were at work, hovering around bass fishermen just waiting for a chance to foul them up. While some people didn't believe in spirits, how did they explain the proven fact that it's always the big fish that get away? He told me about fishing one rainy night when the air was so filled with physical forces and mystical spirits that he could hardly cast a plug without hitting one and getting a backlash.

I started to tell him his main problem was casting into the wind instead of throwing/downwind. I knew, though, he'd only smile and shrug like he was talking to a small child.

A friend of mine who operates a marina has a huge piece of poster paper on his bulletin board. It carries a running tabulation of fishing excuses. It is now up to No. 251. Anglers read it to collect excuses for when they are needed. They are also encouraged to add new excuses. While 251 excuses may not sound like a lot, the poster has only been up two days.

My personal feeling on excuses is that they should not be used. When an angler makes a mistake, he should have the courage to admit it. If he's not catching fish, he shouldn't blame it on the weather but examine his own angling technique.

For instance, when I am having a rough time, the first thing I want to know is when my partner last went to church. Has he been straying at night, clinch dancing, boozing, and slow-trailing hep women? If so, he may be subject to punishment, and I don't want to have part of it rubbing off on me. Why should I pay for his sins by going fishless?

The basic idea of having a "Dial an Excuse" phone service is a good one. After all, there's a similar service for would-be suicides. The telephones are manned around the clock by compassionate people who care about their fellow man. Every community should have one. I've used them several times right after fishing trips.

Once I even dialed Goodwill and told them if they'd send a truck, they could have all my fishing tackle. Before the truck arrived, I had second thoughts and decided to give fishing one more chance. It was embarrassing when the truck arrived, and I told the driver I was keeping the tackle. I felt so bad that I gave him an armload of my wife's dresses.

When my wife discovered the dresses were missing, I told her she had been repeatedly warned to keep the house locked. It didn't bother her too much. She went out and bought a carload of new dresses, but not at Goodwill prices.

A friend of mine, Tom, and I recently hired a striped bass guide for a day of fishing. I knew Tom's wife had been making him go to church. On the third cast, Tom hung a big striper and worked it close to the boat. When the guide tried to net it, the knot holding the lure gave way.

Shortly afterward, I hooked its mate. As the fish tried to pull line off, the guide yelled, "Ease off the drag. Let her run." I put my thumb on the spool and the line snapped like a .22 cartridge firing.

During a lull in the misfortunes, I explained the "Dial an Excuse" project and asked the guide if he thought it had merit. He scratched his chin and said, "Maybe, but for you two guys, your best bet is "Dial a Prayer."

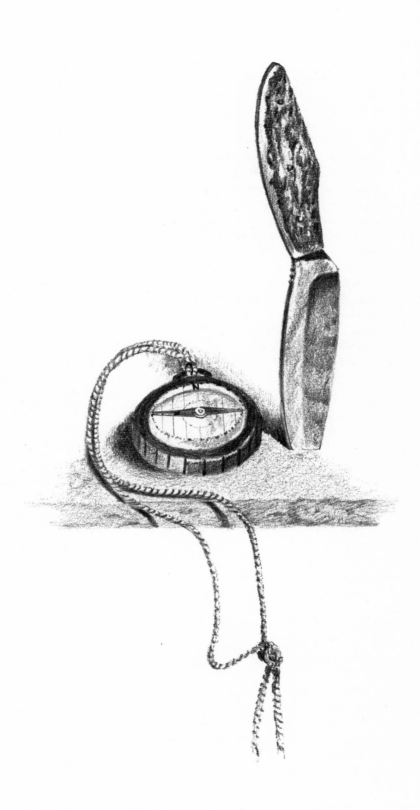

Lines to Exit By

T he hunter learns to fine tune his senses. He listens more carefully when he's outdoors. He recognizes subtle variations in sound, realizing that delicate nuances in pitch, tone, and emphasis carry different meanings.

Many of the noises a hunter hears come from his companions and can best be classified as "famous last words." They are emphatic statements with one meaning meant, but the final results are different, painfully so. The person who makes "famous last words" usually lives to regret them and so do his friends. The following examples may be familiar to you:

"The weatherman says it's not going to rain. Leave your rain gear at home."

"Don't worry about the food this weekend. I'll bring all we will need."

"Poison ivy won't infect you this time of year."

"We'll go back to camp straight across that mountain. It's not nearly as high as it looks."

"The water may be a little low, but my boat will make it through that cut. I've done it a thousand times."

"We'll just leave this pot of stew on the fire all day. When we get back tonight from our deer hunt, dinner will be ready."

"I never bother carrying a compass. I know every tree in this swamp."

"If there's one thing I don't forget, it's the olives."

"Don't worry about it. The game warden never checks our property."

"There's not a mud hole in the state this four-wheeler won't go through."

"Don't worry about those snow clouds. Let's hunt a little longer. The elk are bound to start moving."

"I've been jumping this creek for 30 years."

"No one's ever seen a rattler around here this time of year."

"Forget about taking all that heavy clothing. It never gets cold at our camp this time of year."

"Old John always takes care of bringing the booze."

"The bluebills are just beginning to move. I've never been stranded on a low tide yet."

"Who needs matches? We'll beat two rocks together."

"I always carry too many shells."

"That buck has to fall! I couldn't have missed him three times that close."

"You don't need to pack a lunch. We'll go back to camp for a bite at noon."

"Go on and cross the top of that barbed-wire fence. It may look a little old, but those staples will hold."

"We'll just take our clothes off, hold our rifles up high, and wade across that river. There are no holes in it and hardly any current."

"I always put an extra tank of gas in the duck boat in case we have to run around a lot."

"A little bit of metal, such as guns and knives, doesn't affect a compass enough to worry about."

"You don't have to change out of your good clothes. I just want to ride around and show you some of the feed patches we planted on the floodplain."

"Let's not take any food to camp. It'll be fun living off the land for a week."

"I never miss a pheasant that swings to my left."

"Who needs a topographic map in this country? All you have to do is climb a hill and get a bearing."

"No, I didn't go out to the range. My rifle was still sighted in at the end of last season."

"It's nothing to fill a doe tag. I'll have mine by 8 a.m. tomorrow."

"Just wait until the woodcock begins to level off at the top of its towering."

"No, I don't ask my boss if I can go hunting. I tell him when I'm going."

"Why would anyone need more than three cartridges to take just one buck?"

"I've got that dog to where when he locks up, he's as solid as a rock. You don't have to worry about him busting any birds this season."

"We'll save a lot of time getting back to camp if we cut through that stand of young pines."

"What's so tough about hunting ruffed grouse?"

"That old trail horse has never thrown anybody yet. My little babies ride him all summer."

"I always hang geese for four days before dressing them. I don't think it's that much warmer here."

"Well, buddy, I'll tell you one thing. I don't see how you can miss anything as big as an elk!"

"Boys, just store the food and gear anywhere you want. We never have trouble with bears raiding around here."

"My wife'll look after things. She won't care if I stay a couple of extra days."

A Tough Bottle to Crack

Our federal government is good at thinking up ideas that sound great in theory but are shy of practicality. I wouldn't be surprised if they outlawed fish hooks as hazardous objects, and made it against the law to leave tackle boxes unlocked.

The new childproof tops to medicine bottles are an example of federal minds at their best. There's no way a child can open one of these modern bottles. Neither can an adult, even if he's dying for lack of a pill that's inside. In fact, licensed pharmacists are the only ones who know how to remove the tops.

As much as pills cost these days, you'd think they'd be put in a bottle that would let you get to them when you need one. With most of the cap designs on the market, you could be embalmed by the time it takes to open a bottle.

Recently, I was fishing with Tod Harnett. As always happens when someone is catching more bass than I am, I developed a migraine headache. Because this is a common affliction from March through October, I always carry a bottle of headache tablets.

I took the bottle from my tackle box and started to line up the two invisible arrows before I realized my reading glasses were at home. Thinking that surely the pill makers must allow for adults with uncertain vision, I thought it would be easy to remove the cap by Braille.

After fumbling with the lid and bottle for several minutes, I decided to take the cap off with brute force. That's when I discovered that caps and bottles are the strongest materials on earth.

In desperation, I put the bottle on the bottom of the boat and stomped it with my clodhoppers. I succeeded in denting the bottom of the boat but not in opening the bottle.

Tod, who had been patiently watching, asked if he could help, saying, "Surely any adult of reasonable intelligence can open that bottle."

Soon, he was to regret that statement.

After wrestling the top and bottle all the way from stern to bow, Tod took out his heavy knife and whacked at the lid. I encouraged him by saying over and over, "Surely any adult of reasonable intelligence can open that bottle."

Nothing gave except Tod's temper. If anything good came out of the situation, it was the new expressions Tod used that I added to my vocabulary.

When he grabbed the anchor and began flailing at the bottle, I knew something was going to give. Unfortunately, it was a couple of seat braces but not the cap.

I told Tod we better go ashore before we destroyed the boat. No sooner had we beached than Tod reached in one of the rod compartments and brought out a double-barrel shotgun.

Tod put the bottle on a nearby oak stump and tried to smash it with the butt of his gun stock. It didn't make a dent in the bottle or cap, but it did crack Tod's custom walnut stock.

Foaming from each side of his mouth, Tod grabbed the bottle, walked a few feet from the stump and wound up like a baseball pitcher. He let go with his best fast ball. The new bottles must have a lot of bounce because this one came back at his head like a line drive.

I started to get a bandage for the cut over Tod's eye, but then I stopped. I probably couldn't open that container either, and it would just double our problem.

I knew that my bird dog, Willie, could crack the cap on that bottle in one chomp, but the trouble with Willie is that anything as small as a pill bottle he takes in one gulp, without chewing.

Tod suggested that I grab Willie, put the cap between his teeth and hold his mouth closed. Then Tod would slam Willie on top of his skull with his gun butt and the cap would crack like a pecan.

I instantly vetoed that idea. I surely didn't want Tod doing any more damage to his custom walnut stock!

Tod sat down on the stump, threw his hat on the ground and said, "Maybe we ought to read the directions on that bottle for taking the cap off?"

"You can't," I said. "Not unless you have a microscope for reading two-point type."

Suddenly I realized that we were not using the power available to us. I jumped back in the boat and found a couple of shells in the watertight compartment. I took the bottle and paced off eight yards. Then I loaded the shotgun, aimed, and fired the right barrel.

There was a huge puff of plastic and powder. Tod shouted that I had underestimated the ballistic potential.

Although I was shooting No. 8 shot through an improved cylinder choke, the pattern had been too tight at only eight paces. Obviously, I should have paced off 21 yards, Tod said. He got carried away with the ballistics of the situation and said if they were worked out properly druggists could give away a shotgun and shells with each purchase so that pill bottles could be easily opened.

Meanwhile, I was crawling around on my hands and knees trying to find a couple of headache pills that hadn't been atomized. I suddenly noticed, though, that I no longer had a headache.

In fact, I felt great! Blowing that pill bottle to smithereens sure made me feel good!

Whether 'tis Nobler to Shoot

There are more ways to miss a turkey than there are ways to hit one. You can miss them by not being in the same woods as easily as you can miss with your shotgun. Or you can miss a whole season by letting work interfere with more important things.

Spring gobblers are not tolerant of your mistakes. It doesn't matter which particular mistake you make. If you make just one, you lose and the gobbler wins.

Some of the things that bother me about gobbler hunting are the unanswered ethical and moral questions. The gobbler, responding to an inner drive to perpetuate his species, is lured within shotgun range by a hunter using a call to imitate a sexy hen. The male turkey, under the stimulant of compelling hormones, puffs his chest, fans his tail, extends his wings, and struts forward to make love to a comely hen. In all his glorious finery he strides majestically through the woods to greet his new ladylove. Instead, he is greeted by a blast from a full-choke shotgun. From an ethical standpoint, is this fair?

If you think so, then obviously you have not imagined yourself in the gobbler's situation, or ever been in a similar one in your life.

I realize that raw sex is the easiest way for a hunter to pull a spring gobbler within shotgun range. But there is something vaguely disturbing about shattering the gobbler's hopes so suddenly. He is enticed by the caller to a peak of expectations, and then *kerblam!*

It is easy, of course, to say the gobbler is to blame and gets only what he deserves. It is his fault in the first place. If he had not advertised his sexual availability at daylight by gobbling from his roost, the hunter would not have known he was there.

If the gobbler had quietly sat in his tree and silently flown down for an early-morning romance, no one but he and the hen ever would have known. The gobbler had to broadcast. He not only advertised from his roost, but after flying down he bragged to the whole woods.

There are those who say the gobbler deserves his comeuppance because he is promiscuous. He does not seek a lasting and meaningful relationship with a respectable hen, but settles for the first saucy female that comes along. He no sooner consummates their project than he is tired of her and ready for another hen.

The gobbler is a sexual glutton, and greedy about the whole business. He wants sole breeding rights for a large territory and is unwilling to share the refreshments with lesser gobblers. A harem of five lovely hens is not enough. If he sees a sixth, he will try to collect her.

It means nothing to the old gobbler that a younger fraternal gobbler does not have even one hen. The old boy wants them all, whether or not he can accommodate them.

The main purpose of the gobbler is to get as wide a distribution of his genes as is turkishly possible. Then after working hard at it for a month, he deserts the hens and does nothing to help them rear the chicks. The little chicks grow up without a father, and the old gobbler could care less. While the poults are struggling to survive, the old man is off with a fraternal group of gobblers, probably swapping sex stories.

You may well ask what all of this has to do with spring gobbler hunting. Well, I worry about it a lot.

When I am alone in the woods trying to lure a gobbler, there are times when a tom loudly starts toward me and then there is sudden silence. For an hour or more, I don't know if the gobbler has turned away or is simply circling to sneak in from the rear. That's when I think about ethical and moral questions. After all, one has to think about something.

Locking your mind on deep subjects, such as ethics, can cause you to miss an opportunity to terminate a turkey. Lost in the philosophy of turkey social behavior, you look up and there's a gobbler strutting in a sunny spot 40 yards away. Your mind is slow snapping back to practical reality and making the decision to shoot. Your body is slow and clumsy in raising the shotgun and pointing it. Suddenly the turkeys lowered wings and spread feathers instantly retract into a streamlined racer that vanishes before you can pull the trigger.

As I said at the start, there are a lot of ways you can miss a gobbler. One spring morning along the Pearl River in Mississippi, I had a perfect blind of three fallen pines that formed a small triangle. It was possible to move about, stretch a bit, and yelp without being seen by approaching turkeys. I was sweet-talking a distant gobbler when I heard a *kuhthoom* to my right.

An old gobbler, with five admiring hens, was puffing his chest and generally showing off. I doubt if he had come to gather me as the sixth hen for his harem. It was more likely that he had strolled my way because there was good light spraying through the open pine woods that would show his brilliant plumage to better advantage.

I eased my 28-inch full-choke barrel across the top of a log and pointed the muzzle just down the neck from the glistening blue, bald skull of the gobbler at a range of 35 yards. Just as I started to pull the trigger, though, I noticed a hen behind the tom directly in the line of fire. I eased my finger off the trigger and waited.

Then I saw that an urgent hen was outrageously flirting with the gobbler, shamelessly so in front of the other four hens.

Apparently the hen had received no attention that morning. There was no way of knowing how much satisfaction the gobbler had received from the other hens. Under the circumstances, it did not seem fair to shoot the gobbler until the act of love had been completed.

The act itself took only an instant. It seemed like a lot of foreplay on the gobbler's part to me for such a short payoff. He had been gobbling, fanning, strutting, blowing, and promenading since sunup, but when he finally got down to action it was all over in an instant. That gave me a lot to ponder, in addition to the ethics and morality of shooting the gobbler at this unsuspecting moment. The old boy would never have a chance to tell his fraternal group about his fifth hen.

That put me to wondering how I would feel under the same circumstances. (It required all of the imagination I could muster.) Before I could work out the details, the distant gobbler I had been calling earlier strutted into the piney boudoir.

He was an ancient scrawny gobbler with a beard so long he almost stepped on it with each ponderous step. He lowered his head, puffed his chest, and cupped his wings. When he charged the first gobbler, I knew he could use those long spurs.

I realized that I should quickly shoot the older gobbler and collect what would be a record beard for me. Then I got to thinking; I could not help but wonder if the older gobbler was more interested in fighting or making love, or if he won the fight how soon he would make love.

The scrawny old gobbler's wattles were so red they were about to bust.

His shrunken head turned from blue to white and on his first charge there was no sparring. He bowled the larger turkey over and before that tom could get back up, the old warrior jumped three feet in the air and thrust his legs out. He landed on the back of the first gobbler with spurs jabbing.

Spring gobblers don't usually fight to kill another male—they just want him to leave so they can breed in peace. Anyone can identify with this. The scrawny gobbler was an exception. He had blood in his eye and death in his spurs. The first gobbler tucked in his feathers and scooted out of there. I started to shoot the inferior retreating gobbler, but then balked. I got to wondering what the scrawny old gobbler would do now that he was chief pistol in a new harem.

Well, first of all, he acted like there was nothing to it. He was almost modest, as if it was old hat to whip a larger gobbler every morning before breakfast.

During the brief fight, the hens hadn't paid much attention, some of them plucking at early green shoots and one chasing a grasshopper. This caused me to realize that hens are as promiscuous as males. They had just lost a gobbler they had been keeping company and consummating with, and they didn't care enough to lose their appetites for a second.

While I was reflecting on the fickleness of females, the scrawny gobbler led his new harem to a different part of his kingdom. Then it occurred to me that I had failed to shoot a gobbler that morning.

When I told the story back at camp, the other hunters weren't much help. One was unkind enough to suggest that I could think about the ethics of turkey hunting 11 months a year, but I'd be better off dropping the subject while the season was open.

I told them that if they were ever going to develop a philosophy of spring-gobbler hunting, it was vital to consider the ethics and morals. A hunter, who had just finished plucking a young tom, said that I could eat all the philosophy I wanted for supper, but the rest were going to enjoy roast turkey. I don't hold out much hope of him ever becoming a well-rounded turkey hunter.

A couple of years ago, I hunted spring gobblers with Ben Rodgers Lee in Gees Bend alongside the Alabama River. Ben had built me an enclosed blind in a small chufa field surrounded by woods. The chufas had gotten through the winter without the deer and turkeys digging them up. The field was not only a good place for turkeys to feed, but also for gobblers to strut.

Ben didn't tell me one thing about the blind. He had been removing skunks and had set a trap about 10 yards from the blind. When he dropped me off about an hour before daylight, there was a skunk in the trap. It was not a happy skunk and had made its displeasure known by liberally saturating the area.

Ben said that turkeys didn't mind skunk odor and that after a while I wouldn't notice it either. Besides, it was a good spot and there wasn't time to build a blind in another area. I had a pocket camera along and hoped to take pictures after I bagged a gobbler. The turkeys were used to this blind, but they'd be jumpy about a new one.

Before the sun peeked over the horizon, a gobbler began advertising from his roost 200 yards away. A hen came gliding in over the treetops and landed in the chufa field. I instantly realized I had a perfect setup. If the hen did any yelping, she'd pull in the gobbler and I wouldn't have to call.

The hen had barely landed when she realized something was wrong. She spotted the skunk and knew it wasn't acting right. She came striding across the field and walked almost up to it, chattering away. The skunk, which had an unusually large storage tank, raised its tail and sprinkled several gallons. It was just as Ben said—skunk scent doesn't bother turkeys! The wisp of wind was coming in my direction, though. The essence of skunk quickly invaded my entire respiratory system. I held my nose with one hand and put the other over my mouth to muffle the gasping.

As the sun got higher, the gobbler pealed one commercial after another. I was sure that he could hear the chattering hen, but she was not giving out any lovesick yelps. Then I noticed huge shadows moving across the field. I looked up to see a dozen buzzards that had discovered the skunk's plight.

They circled lower and lower, and finally one got up the nerve to land and flop toward the hen turkey. Apparently the hen thought she had certain rights concerning the skunk because she got into a wing-flapping fight with the buzzard. At that moment, the gobbler landed in the field. He took one look at the situation and charged in, with head and neck extended and wings dragging.

All this was happening only 10 yards from me. When the gobbler skidded to a halt in front of the skunk, he paused to survey the situation. He didn't know whether to attack the skunk, make love to the hen, or run the buzzard off. I couldn't make a decision on whether to reach for my shotgun or try to quietly get my camera and take a picture.

Then my thoughts began to drift. If the turkey hen decided to leave, would the romantic gobbler try to mate with the buzzard? First of all, I didn't know how to tell a male from a female buzzard, but I was sure the gobbler could. Or perhaps, in the gobbler's excited state, it wouldn't make any difference. Then I wondered what the reaction of the buzzard would be—receptive or resentful?

At that instant, my throat had all of the tickling from skunk scent it could stand. I went into a severe coughing spasm, which almost took the roof off the blind. When I carefully peeked out, the field was deserted except for the unhappy skunk.

Figuring the skunk had dehydrated itself, I left my blind and freed it. Then I walked a half mile to unpolluted air and waited for Ben to arrive in his pickup. When Ben, a world-champion turkey caller, picked me up, I told him the story.

He shook his head and said, "When you get a chance at a gobbler you had better take it. And take it in a hurry!"

"Well," I replied, "that may be true. But I can't spend the rest of my life trying to explain how a skunk called up a spring gobbler for me to shoot."

Besides, I didn't have time to work out the ethics of the situation.

The Long and Short of It

There is one constant law at hunting camps to which there are no exceptions. Thousands of hunters try to escape the law each year, but none is successful. No technology, cleverness, or conjuring enables the hunter to evade the powers of the law.

Stated simply, the law says that no man can look dignified in a suit of long underwear. Regardless of physique, breeding, training, or social position, no hunter looks dignified clad only in long handles. A judge sitting in black-robed dignity in his courtroom inspires respect, but, let him waddle around a hunting camp in long underwear, and smiles, chuckles, or belly laughs will follow his steps.

In the old days, when long handles were one piece with the famous trapdoor, there was no hope for a hunter who appeared before his buddies to retain his natural dignity. The underwear rolled at the arm and leg openings, buckled at the knees, and sagged at the crotch like an unpegged tent in the wind. The back-door buttons were forever disappearing and the flap was as unstable as smoke rising from a campfire.

With the coming of two-piece union suits, clothing designers made a stab at style. New materials took out some of the canyons and overthrusts. They have never been able to overcome the revealing nature of stretched cloth, though. There is honesty in long underwear. It reveals the flaws and faults of the body underneath.

You, yourself, have seen it at camp. A slender executive of middle age wears a tailored business suit as though he were a professional clothes model. At camp, however, when he warms himself before a fire and is clad only in long handles, his imperfections are obvious for all to see. No one ever suspected he had a rolling paunch and skinny legs. How does he have the strength to hunt on those spindly legs that would look better on a crane?

One does not, of course, become the target of too many stale jokes when one appears in long handles unless one tries to hide one's own malformities. Although no word is spoken, there is a quiet understanding that all of us have flaws, that perhaps even stay obvious when camouflaged by outer garments.

It is permissible to poke good-natured fun at a companion's spreading hip bulges, but, if you do it unkindly, he's liable to describe your shortcomings in great detail.

Sometimes hunters, keenly aware of their pregnant look, put on long handles the first night in camp, parade around for all to see, and get their exposure over with. Many years ago, at the Burnt Beans Baldpate Duck Club, the highlight of the annual seasonal opening was the appearance of Randy Bartow.

If he had been a little taller, he would have been built like a beer barrel. He had the girth for it. There was no way he could look anything but ridiculous in a union suit, and he knew it. The only hope for him was to have some fun with the situation. Following a generous priming of the pump, he dressed in his oldfashioned long handles, with the barn door wide open, and pirouetted into the main room with his famous "Dance of Spring."

Following his opening number, Randy gave his interpretation of how the ballet *Swan Lake* should be danced. After we recovered from our hysterical laughter, there was nothing more said about Randy's appearance.

When Randy passed on to that great waterfowl refuge in the sky, the club voted that his membership be filled by G. Parker Worthington, a newcomer to our community. He was of medium stature, efficient, an excellent shot, and in love with himself. On the first weekend, we realized he didn't quite fit in with our membership. You might say he was pompous.

If you mentioned shooting a baldpate at 45 yards, he told about shooting one at 60 yards. If a hunter tried to tell about a double, G. Parker broke in to brag about a triple. When one of the boys mentioned a good hunt on Round Lake in the next county, he didn't get to finish because G. Parker interrupted to tell about his hunt in Patagonia.

About the fourth weekend, old Slim Roberts, the club's senior member, called several of us together and said, "Boys, we got to do something about this G. Parker. He's basically a nice guy, but he's missing humility."

We agreed to let Slim take care of the matter in his own way. What he did first was to slip into G. Parker's room and check the size and brand of his long handles. G. Parker wore medium, so when Slim got back to town he bought pairs of men's extra large and boy's small in the same brand. Then he ran them through the laundry machine.

The next weekend included a holiday, so most of us went to camp for four days. A front out of Canada roared in, and the chill factor dropped to "Maybe I should stay in bed."

That night the air was blue and we all decided to sleep in our long handles. Slim had switched G. Parker's mediums with the pair of boy's small.

We heard some mumbling and grumbling from G. Parker's room, and then he came yelling out to the fire looking like a half-plucked chicken. The bottoms of the legs were up around his knees, the sleeves were at his elbows, and his crotch was cinched up in a stranglehold. We fell on the floor laughing.

For the next four mornings, G. Parker's long handles were either dragging the floor or cutting off his breath. When he took a nap before the afternoon hunts or work parties, Slim changed the long handles again. Just to keep G. Parker off balance, he sometimes got to wear his own underwear. We giggled like school kids at whatever he wore. It was all funny to us.

G. Parker lost his dignity, composure, and poise, but he saved his membership. He turned out to be one of our best members, though on the quiet side for a year or two.

Mister Willie

The trouble with becoming partners with a bird dog is that one day he'll up and die on you. You know that going in, but it doesn't make it any easier when it finally happens.

Willie, my nine-year-old setter companion, recently died peacefully while stretched out sleeping. It was his favorite position and he seemed to have a grin on his orange-spotted face. There's no doubt that dogs dream, and I like to think Willie was pointing a tight-holding covey of bobwhite quail as he left this world.

You can always get another hunting dog as a partner, but there's no way to get one, good or bad, exactly like the one you've lost. Each dog is as much an individual as a person is, and when you lose one there's no replacement.

I remember trying to console a dog owner several years ago who had lost an old partner. There's really not much you can say about death to cheer anyone up and all I know to do is try and express sympathy. On this occasion, wanting to communicate understanding, I said, "Losing a good bird dog is almost as bad as losing your wife, isn't it?"

The hunter, his eyes misty with tears, slowly shook his head and stared at me. Finally he said, "It's worse than that. A whole lot worse!"

When my wife found Willie, he was lying in one of his favorite spots, a soft rug in the living room where the warmth of the morning sun came through a picture window. It's a good place to watch for the garbage truck, postman, stray dogs, and anything else that needs barking at.

My wife gave a little scream and came running into the den, tears trickling down her cheeks. Most of the time, Willie had been her dog. She insisted on feeding him, giving him his pills, and pulling stickums out of his silky feathers. Willie liked her better than he did me most of the year. He could more easily con her. During the hunting season, however, he favored me. He was afraid I'd take the other setters and leave him at home.

After my wife and I calmed down a bit, we tried to face the reality of Willie's departure. We knew the worst shock of his leaving would come later.

My wife suggested that I take Willie's body to the vet for cremation. That didn't seem right to me, so I told her that I was going to bury Willie in the front yard. She said I couldn't do that because it was against a city ordinance.

I shouted, "To hell with the city," and headed for the garage to get a shovel. Death makes some of us angry, mainly because it's so final and there's nothing we can do about it. I was upset but still clear-headed enough to hope no neighbor or cop would interfere with Willie's burial. I was afraid that I might take a swing at them with the shovel.

It took an hour to dig a hole wide and deep enough for Willie's lank frame. It was just outside the picture window between two bushes. These were favorite bushes when I took Willie outside at night for a search around the front yard. It was important for him to sniff around and find out how many squirrels and dogs had invaded his territory. He always sprayed those bushes a couple of times to inform future trespassers that they were on Willie's turf.

I gently placed Willie in the hole, but it was all I could do to throw the dirt on him to cover him. It was some consolation that Willie's spot would get the morning sun, a place to see the garbage truck long before it reached our house. But not much.

I don't know anything about dog heaven. Maybe there isn't one, but there ought to be. Perhaps they use ours? That's a logical system because no bird-dog man can imagine a heaven without pointing dogs to train and hunt.

Whatever the situation, I'm pretty sure Willie made it. The good book cites the case of the prodigal son. Willie was a sinner and frequently squandered his birthright. He would show signs of guilt and remorse, though, when he transgressed. At times, he almost seemed to apologize. That never kept him from repeating the same sins.

Willie was sure he knew more about hunting birds with gamy smells—

quail, woodcock, and grouse—than I did. In fact, he didn't accept the notion that I knew anything at all and always hunted where he pleased. He had hearing problems. If I wanted him to work some area he didn't want to comb, Willie went deaf. If I whispered, "Goodie, goodie," a sound that meant he was about to be given a tasty tidbit, he could hear me a mile away.

His nose was so keen that you couldn't tell if he was working toward a covey or backtracking. He'd pick up scent that two dogs running ahead had crossed and never smelled. If he got sore about something, though, he'd leave and go back to the Jeep. Once, when he was doing fine in the field, he got mad and quit because I whipped another dog. Willie walked at heel the rest of the afternoon. He had as many complexes as a conference full of psychologists.

If there was a cow pie to roll in, Willie would find it just before you were ready to load up. On a grouse trip in Michigan, Willie found his first porcupine. He circled it barking and got a younger dog excited enough to attack it and end up with a mouthful of quills. Willie didn't get a barb.

He seldom lived up to his potential. If he was hunting with another hunter's bitch, he'd follow her all day, even if she wasn't in heat. If he saw another hunting party, he'd leave me and join them. He had the ability to be a fine bird dog, but he usually got distracted. On one of the last hunts he went on, there were four dogs and Willie showed what he could do. There were 11 finds of bobwhite coveys and Willie was the first to point nine of them. This was only a month after his first heart attack. It's the hunt I'll always try to remember when I think of him.

Willie was reasonably tolerant of my misses and other mistakes. I always forgave Willie of his sins. There was nothing else to do; you couldn't change him. Now, if I could just have him back, I wouldn't want to change him. I'd gladly take him any way I could get him.

Old Masters

If you don't know some dukes, barons, or other people with steady work, Europe isn't a good place to go hunting. I just got back from a trip over there and what I did mostly was follow my wife through a lot of old churches. She says the more old churches you go through, the more cultured you get.

I'd have liked to shoot a few of the pigeons, but those birds make up the main wildlife for most Europeans. The trouble with ending up in places such as Paris and not being able to hunt is that there's not much to do. That's why they must keep restoring so many old buildings—so the natives and tourists have something to do.

Because I couldn't get lined up to go hunting around Paris, I decided to look for sporting prints and originals. A cab racer took us to some place called "The Louvre," which has a lot of pictures. It's a rambling old building considerably eroded by carbon monoxide, but Europeans prefer things that look as if they came off Noah's ark.

I started in the basement with the Grecian section. There wasn't much light and everyone was gathered around a damaged statue in the middle of the room. A Chinese man told me it was named Venus de Milo.

Both arms were knocked off and Venus was chipped in a lot of places. I'll bet those Frenchmen were sure mad when she arrived. They must have shipped her by the same airline that always snaps my gun cases.

The Louvre had a lot of whole statues that were not broken up, but they were mostly in poor light. I guess they put Venus out in the open to get back at the airline. They also might have figured they had a better chance of selling her that way, but I don't guess a busted-up statue would bring much.

It takes an American awhile to get used to all of the naked statues indoors and out in Paris. Nearly every park I saw was filled with naked statues, and the carvers didn't leave any anatomy to your imagination. Tourists stop and stare at the details, but the Frenchmen are used to bare statues and I never saw one take a second look, or even a first for that matter. All the old Greek statues that depicted hunting had people shooting bows or hurling plates.

In the old Dutch section of The Louvre there was a lot of big pictures that looked familiar. At first I thought it was because of my courses in art appreciation, but then I remembered that a lot of the pictures were used on Dutch Masters cigar boxes.

There are blue-coated guards all over The Louvre. When I asked one if The Louvre had to pay royalties to the Dutch Masters Company, he gave me a shrug.

Not even an Italian can shrug as eloquently as a Frenchman. A shrug means several things or a combination of them: 1) It is not my fault; 2) Who can say?; 3) That's life; or 4) Forget it!

Whenever I asked about a place near Paris to go hunting, all I ever got was a shrug. Of course, they might not have understood the accent of my French, especially since I don't know any French.

The skinny female models of today sure couldn't have gotten a job when some painter named Reubens was around. There wasn't a rib showing on those corn-fed girls he painted, but everything else was.

I guess those old painters were poor and kept running out of draping material. In a lot of the pictures, the men had plenty of clothes, but the women barely had any. I asked my wife about that and she said all the male models were probably hunters and spent all their money on new guns they didn't need so there was never enough left over for the wives.

In one huge room with 12 large paintings, six had one or more naked people and the other six had models with clothes on. I guess that's the French system of giving people a choice to look at whatever they want to see. Or maybe their supreme court can't make up its mind either.

There weren't many hunting and fishing pictures that I could find. An artist named A. Van Dyke had a big picture called "Charles 1st Roi d'Angleterre." The French aren't good spellers and spell Henry "Henri" and Roy "Roi."

Anyway, old Charles 1st Roi wore a cocked cap and was posing in full strut. Although there was no gun showing, it was obvious from his expression that he had just made a double on pheasants and was waiting for any and all compliments.

There was a riprap dog in one of Reubens's paintings that looked as if it might have some pointer blood. There were about 20 people in the painting, all in trauma of some degree, and it was obvious that bidding for the dog had been high and bitter.

There was a big crowd around a small picture called "The Mona Lisa," even though she had plenty of clothes on. I thought Mona had sneaky eyes. They followed you wherever you went. She would have been good to hang over the refreshments at deer camp when you got down to the last bottle or two.

I couldn't find out who the artist was that painted Mona, but it must have been somebody important to attract so much attention and so many spectators.

There were no price tags listed below any of the pictures so I figured it'd cost a bundle to buy one. At least that's the way it was in those cafés that didn't have prices listed on their menus.

Before we went back to the States, we stopped in Holland. With all of the canals and channelization it was easy to tell the U.S. Army Corps of Engineers had been there. We got some more culture by racing through old churches and museums that looked pretty much the same as those we'd seen in France.

One of the best things about taking my wife is that I've done my good deed for the year and built up all the free time I can handle for the rest of the hunting season.

By the Light of the Silvery Moon

Some anglers believe so strongly in solunar tables they fish at no other times than those which the charts indicate. Maybe they spend less time not catching fish than other anglers do.

Have you ever seen a fisherman stay home on the morning of the trout opener because the solunar tables indicated a better time later on? Another point: No matter what the tables say for Saturday and Sunday, on Friday morning all fishermen say, "Thank goodness, it's Friday."

Fishermen have been arguing for years over how much affect, if any, the positions of the sun and moon have on when fish feed. The late President John F. Kennedy apparently got interested in the problem and the government spent a lot of money sending Neil Armstrong all the way to the moon. He didn't catch any fish, though, or get anything settled.

I have spent considerable time on both fresh and salt water, but I have never seen a fish stick its head out and take a bearing on the moon or sun. If a fish gets hungry, it goes looking for a handy source of food and lets anglers worry about solunar tables.

I can't ever remember checking the moon phase before deciding to raid the icebox. A boring television show is more apt to make me run to the pantry than is the gravitational pull of the moon.

For the sake of scientific objectivity, I kept a log of my icebox raids for three months and plotted them on a graph in relationship to solunar tables. The results showed that I had a major feeding period every night between 10 and 11 p.m. with a minor feeding period after the late news.

The nightly consumption was not geared to the solunar tables. There was, however, a direct correlation with whether the news was good or bad. Because there's seldom any good news on the tube, I was often still nibbling crackers when I climbed into bed.

Our English setter, Rat, does not feed by the solunar tables. He runs to the kitchen whenever he hears a can being opened, an icebox door clicking, or any sort of pan rattling. His major feeding period is whenever he can find anything edible that is smaller than he is.

You have to be careful at our home. If you drop a piece of food, you better not reach for it. It's hard to walk around with your hand in Rat's stomach.

People who swear by the solunar tables don't realize what they're saying. You could give them a sun and moon fix, a set of trig tables, and a ream of paper and they still couldn't figure out in a week the relative positions of sun, moon, and earth.

Yet, some people say a fish does it with no effort—sort of automatically. What they're really saying is that a fish has more sense than a fisherman! Well, come to think of it . . . .

There's a new Solar-Lunar plotting grid on the market. It's made of plastic and is a handy size for your hip-pocket or tackle box. You set a couple of dials and instantly read the major and minor feeding periods for any day in the year.

I've found this calculator of tremendous help with my fishing. It enables me to eliminate all the days which have major feeding hours at horrible times like 5 a.m.

I like major feeding periods when they're about 10 a.m. You don't have to get up early but the wind is usually still down. I stay out until one of *my* major feeding periods—noon. No solunar table is needed to inform me that this major activity should be followed by a siesta.

Of course, I believe the moon affects life forms. Rat consistently howls at the full moon. So does one of my neighbors, but he ties his own flies. I guess the ones that slip in under the screen door aren't good enough for him.

At home, I watch the birds and squirrels in the yard. If they become active, I grab my fishing gear and rush to the nearest lake. It's not that I expect the fish to be active. I just hate to fill the feeders in the yard.

A friend of mine receives cattle reports from a farmer. If the cows become restless and then start to feed, the farmer phones. My friend jumps in his car and races for the farm pond. His theory is that cows and fish react on the same timetable. It's a good theory except the cows are fat, but my friend has caught only one fish. It happened one hot day when the cows went into the pond to cool off and scared a bass up on the bank.

I have a standing order with the same farmer. He's to call me if he ever sees the cows lying down and then getting up by first straightening their front legs and then their hind legs. When that happens, something unusual is bound to be going on. Maybe the fish will even hit.

I have a fishing buddy who's struck by each full moon. He fishes a farm pond all night for three nights either side of the full moon and believes he's going to catch the new world-record bass. He's already caught one that weighed three pounds! It doesn't bother him. He says he only has 19 pounds to go.

He may break the record! He owns more than 300 different lures, an Aztec sundial, a Rosetta stone in the original Greek, and belongs to the Ancient Mystic Order Rosae Crucis. He has his own sextant, is taking astronomy at night school, and just about has Einstein's Theory of Relativity whipped. One of these days he's liable to put it all together when conditions are perfect. I think his chances would improve, however, if he'd quit casting to the bank and would concentrate on that deep hole in the middle.

The Red Revival

W hen you see a friend every week or so, you don't notice his aging, but if you're away from him for several months, you notice a big difference when you come back.

Last autumn it was hard to tell how Red Parsons had gotten his nickname so many years before. His red hair had turned solid white and shone like the sun hitting a set of highly rubbed antlers. Too many hours of unrelenting sun on a tender skin had wrinkled the back of his neck into ridges and valleys like the hide of an old terrapin.

He had taught most of us how to handle an incoming dove with a shotgun or helped us graduate from a .22 rimfire to a big-bore rifle. We knew that he had slipped past his three score and ten, and outward signs of weathering were natural. It wasn't Red's outward appearance that had his old hunting buddies worried, though. It was the inward signs that concerned us.

He started making excuses not to go on dove hunts. At first he explained by saying, "You boys go ahead. I've shot my share." He didn't fool anybody. We knew he was proud of his shooting, but his tired eyes could no longer distinguish the birds that flew below the treeline and blurred out. The only doves Red could see to shoot were those that were silhouetted against the sky. Red had always taken the birds as they came in. He couldn't adjust to shooting only the blue-sky shots. That seemed sort of like cheating.

Red quit taking his afternoon walks of a couple miles, and everyone noticed the lenses on his glasses were thicker. He spent too much time in front of a television set and, when a show was over, he couldn't tell you what it was about. The leaves piled up in his yard, and I noticed a couple of rifles hanging in his den were beginning to get flecks of rust. He talked too long and often spoke about his wife's passing three years back.

Nobody seemed to know how Red spent his time. With deer season rolling around, our old club members got together to exchange stories and scouting information. It looked like a record crop of acorns, and the big bucks would be in the hardwood bottoms. Red never showed up for any of the socializing and, when we stopped by, didn't seem to care what the deer were doing.

Well, we all decided Red was going hunting on opening day and we got together and built a tree stand as big as a king-size bed, with a railing and a stool for sitting. The legs had rubber caps so that, when Red scooted it, there wouldn't be any squeaks.

We didn't put a ladder up to the stand. Carny Davis, a contractor, got a whole set of stairs out of a building he tore down and attached them to the stand steady as a granite mountain, banisters and all. The deer had two weeks to get used to it before opening day, but Carny said he wanted to help the situation along, so he bought about $50 worth of doe urine and saturated the whole stand.

I felt bad about the way we had to browbeat Red into sighting in his rifle, cleaning up his gear, and getting ready for opening day. He made all kinds of excuses why he couldn't go and finally blurted out that he just couldn't see well enough to shoot anymore. We had him sitting in that stand an hour before daylight, though, with his favorite .270 bolt-action rifle.

About the time the first orange peeked through the bare trees, I heard Red's rifle crack once. I was about a quarter of a mile away, and fast-walked to his stand.

Red whispered down, "A big buck, about 225 yards across that wheat field. I shot for his heart but I don't know whether I got him or clean missed."

I'm a generation younger than Red, so I took off at a fast pace on the bearing he gave me. When I reached the edge of the field and woods, I saw a big mound of brown and white. The buck was drilled right through the heart and had as pretty a 10-point rack as I ever saw come out of the woods.

I waved to Red and jumped up and down. Then I dogtrotted across the field back to the stand. When I told Red he had hit the big buck just where he had aimed, and how large the antlers were, I thought he was going to slide down the tree like it was a firepole.

As we hurried toward the buck, Red was talking a mile a minute. He told me how the buck crashed into the field, head low as though following a doe, and then stopped to survey his kingdom. Red's eyes were twinkling and he was carrying that bolt-action rifle in his hands like it weighed only two pounds!

Well, one by one for the next couple of hours, our boys came up and Red told each one exactly how he had estimated the range at 225 yards, held an inch high, and gently squeezed the trigger.

Our state has liberal deer regulations, and a hunter can take three bucks. The next morning, Red, who seemed to have forgotten about his eyesight, was back up in his palace stand. Shortly after sunup, he shot a six-pointer at 255 yards. I'm pretty sure of the distance, because he made several of us step it off.

A few days later, a delegation of old hunting friends called on me and said I had been elected to talk to Red. Something had to be done about him! He was out jogging at noon every day, he'd bought two new rifles, had sighted both in on his TV set with live ammo, and was singing around the house so loud it had the neighborhood dogs barking. On top of that, he'd been out sparking the Widow Barton, and the two of them were planning to go rock-and-rolling at a juke on Saturday night. If somebody didn't do something, the darned old fool was going to kill himself!

Setting the Pace

N o one knows how long a pace is, especially hunters. A pace is some indefinite linear distance between one inch and as much as a metric yard. Hunters use a pace as a system of expressing distance, such as how far a dove fell or the distance to a buck from the shooter's position.

Hunters know that a pace is an inexact expression of distance, but they like it. The reason they use it is because there's an implication that a pace is a yard. Because no hunter ever paces a full yard, or anywhere close to it, the use of the term "pace" makes the hunter appear more skilled. His shots, as told by him, are always on the long side.

When telling stories, hunters instinctively know when to be exact and when to use vague terms. A hunter can be technical and scientific when explaining how he loaded his cartridges. When it comes to how far away the game was taken, though, the hunter drifts off into vague terms.

If you think I'm being a little hard on hunters you just stop and think back on how many hunters you have ever seen carry a tape measure into the field. In fact, how often have you taken a tape so that you could come up with a precise measurement yourself?

It's true that conditions of cover and terrain might not make it easy to tape a 200-yard shot. It's also true that wavering conditions of transit caused by cover and terrain may result in a 300-yard shot when it's paced off.

There is not much glory in a 50-yard shot at a mule deer with a telescopic sight and modern rifle. Hunters know that it sounds much better when telling a story if the buck was shot at 100 yards. That's why so many bucks are shot at 400 yards!

It isn't that hunters deliberately lie. They just want to please the listener, so they oblige him by making it an unusual and interesting story, such as dropping a buck at 600 paces.

After awhile, the hunter telling the same story quits using the term "pace" and uses "long paces" or "yards." By the next season, he actually believes he killed a buck at 800 yards. By the following season, the buck "was running wide open at a half mile when I shot. I paced it off with real long, stretching strides to be sure I stayed on the conservative side."

Some hunters, when measuring distance to fallen birds, can't walk a straight line in a flat stubble field. They weave all over the place and a 35-yard shot ends up with a mourning dove having been shot at 60 yards. A friend of mine takes his two-year-old son to the dove field. When the old man knocks a bird down, he says, "Come on, Junior, you pace off the distance to Daddy's bird."

The kid is in great demand by other hunters, especially because he's a waddler and can't see straight and falls back one step every time he takes two. The old man pays for his shells by renting the kid out for short surveying work.

You may think this is an exaggeration but I have a friend who takes a toy poodle whitewing hunting. It's one of those little foo-foo dogs, and he's decorated in hunter orange so some hunter won't mistake him for a rat and shoot him. Actually, the tiny poodle still has some hunting instinct left in his genes and enjoys going afield.

The foo-foo dog wants to retrieve and always starts toward fallen whitewings. He easily gets deterred from his mission, however. At the dog's height, he can't see over the stubble or maybe he has a poor sense of direction. Anyway, it may take several circles and a lot of false starts before the poodle locates the bird. All the time the dog is frantically searching, the owner is counting steps. Each step is a pace and that's why the owner can brag with a clear conscience that he consistently drops whitewings at 80 yards with a 28-gauge shotgun.

Hunters who tell hunting stories are trapped by the expectations of listeners. Who wants to hear of a dove being shot on the wing at 10 yards? Actually, it was probably a very difficult shot, especially if the bird dove in on you and you were shooting a modified or full-choked shotgun. The pattern at 10 yards for a full-choked shotgun is only about the size of a softball. It was an excellent shot or a lucky one. But it just doesn't sound right at 10 yards.

So the hunter tells about birds dropped at a great distance, such as 60 yards, with the implication that he does it all the time. That has a better ring to it. It's more pleasing to the audience, whether they believe the tale or not.

This factor may influence field systems of measuring. For instance, a gunner may hit a going-away dove at 30 yards but the momentum of the flight carries the bird 30 more yards before it is stopped by the ground. When describing the shot, the hunter doesn't give the distance at which the dove was hit but the distance at which it was picked up.

The opposite system is used for an incomer, a dove flying right at you. If you hit the bird at 30 yards, it may fall at your feet. It wasn't a one-foot shot but actually a full 30-yard shot.

I've known some deer hunters who used the same principle of measuring. They hit a standing buck 50 yards away with an ill-placed shot and the animal runs 400 yards before lying down to die. When the hunter finds the buck, he calls it a 450-yard shot.

If you are going to tell hunting stories, it pays to have a certain part of your memory equipped with an eraser. I have a friend, a great teller of tales, who believes he consistently scores on flying geese at distances of 80 yards. I believe that he may have dropped one goose at 80 yards but I think he has forgotten the 49 other shots at this distance which he missed.

In the first place, he shouldn't have been shooting at this distance because he's only going to cripple birds, assuming his shot string ever comes that close. Secondly, I don't think he knows how far 80 yards really is. For instance, he can't look at a tight parking space between two cars and tell if he can park his own car in between. He drags in a huge stepladder to change a light bulb on an eight-foot ceiling when all he'd have to do is stand on a chair. He thinks the stripes on a football field are 20 yards apart.

On the other hand, if you are going to be a teller of hunting stories, your memory should be good enough so that you tell the same story the same way each time to the same people. That's pretty hard to do over a period of years. If there's anything I hate, it's a person who remembers my stories better than I do.

Only recently, I was telling a group of hunters about making a perfect 150-pace heart shot on a running buck with a handgun a few years back. Old Jim Taylor broke in and said, "That's funny! The buck was 100 paces last year. Three years ago, it was 75 paces. When you got back to camp after shooting the buck that day, you said you shot him at 20 paces and the buck was standing still!"

Well, I never did think much of Jim Taylor and don't know why I ever hunted with him in the first place. He ought to tend to his own hunting stories and leave mine alone!

One of the reasons hunters have been slow in adapting to the metric system is the yard problem. A metric yard is longer than a standard yard. It's not a critical distance but to a hunter it can mount up. A hunter is not in favor of any system which will make his shot sound shorter. Besides, indefinite paces are a natural and preferred system. They give the hunter some stretching room when he goes to relating his brand of victories.

A hunter could, of course, measure the distance of his kills in millimeters. That would really sound big. A millimeter is only .0394 of an inch. The trouble is that listeners are already broken in to paces and know how to adjust to them.

If a hunter I don't know tells me he shot a running buck at 400 long paces, with the implication that it was 400 yards, I automatically adjust the statistic by half. I can believe he shot a buck at 200 yards. At least I can give him that much benefit of the doubt.

There's another adjustment. Have you ever known a hunter who made an allegedly long shot at a standing deer? Well, I don't. The buck was always running wide open or leaping over tall trees or about to disappear in the brush.

When a hunter tells me the distant buck he took was running at full speed, I crank in an adjustment and assume the deer was walking or ambling. With some hunters I know, I give them the benefit of believing that the buck might have been twitching his tail from a standing position.

I know the hunter is doing the best he can to entertain me with his story, in addition to grooming his own ego. The story sounds much better if the deer was shot at the crest of a 30-foot leap rather than while anchored. The storyteller knows I may make adjustments in what I believe. All he wants me to do is keep them to myself. If I want to keep him for a friend, I don't show utter disbelief on my face or snicker and say, "I wouldn't believe that yarn in a million years!"

If a hunter tells me he dropped a running mule deer at 600 long paces with a handgun, he will probably imply that it was skill and he has done it before and could do it any morning before breakfast. He's not going to say it was a lucky shot. Well, I have a multiple reduction adjustment to make.

First of all, I want to remain calm because he has insulted my intelligence if he thinks I'm going to swallow that whole. Then I reduce the distance by a factor of six. He might have taken a buck once in his life at 100 long paces, checked at home with a yardstick later, and perhaps actually 100 true standard yards. The buck was sauntering or standing still, though. The reduction factor of six still applies: when shot he was not running, galloping, jumping, leaping, bounding, or flying.

It isn't that I don't know that hunters sometimes make remarkable shots. It's just that I know hunters.

A friend of mine, who likes to wear a handgun on his belt while hunting with a rifle or shotgun, tells a great story. I have heard it many times and have to congratulate him for being consistent. It seems that he stepped across a sizable log on a warm day and suddenly heard a rattlesnake buzz. He turned in his tracks and instantly realized the snake was preparing to strike. As the snake's head lunged forward, with mouth wide open and fangs extended, he drew his trusty .38 and shot the rattler's head off in mid-strike.

There is a lot that bothers me about that story. First of all, my friend is not well-coordinated and has trouble hitting his mouth with a spoonful of camp beans. He has two deep scars down his right thigh from being out of sync on practice fast draws. That is, he pulled the trigger while the revolver was still in the holster. I will give him a 10 for being persistent.

In addition, no one at camp will let him cut firewood. He has trouble hitting the wood with the ax and is always dulling it by pounding bedrock. Also, we won't let him use the ax because we're afraid he'll hurt himself or cut the tent ropes or break the ax. If you wonder why we allow him to hunt on our lease, we have an answer for that, too. We give him half the lease and the rest of us split up the other half. Then we pray that he stays in his assigned half.

Another factor which bothers me about his snake exploit is that when most people hear a rattler buzz behind them they instantly jump in the opposite direction. They don't stand in their tracks and turn around and look, as he said he did. I realize that when one hears a rattler buzz its first alert the noise sometimes seems to come from all directions. One doesn't at first realize in which direction the rattler lies. Most hunters, though, figure any place is better than the one they're standing in and instantly leap.

Yet, I believe there are elements of truth in my friend's story. I believe that he saw a rattler and I also believe he shot it with his .38 revolver. I'm also inclined to believe he went into shock when he heard the rattler buzz, or quickly afterward. He now believes he drew his revolver and shot the snake's head off as it struck. Under the stress of the moment, one might have all sorts of visions which later seemed real. He believes he shot the rattler's head off in full stroke because that's what his mind registered under trauma. It is a very real and honest memory to him. Anyway, he's willing to fight anybody who makes fun of his rattlesnake story.

Snake stories, whether anyone is under stress or not, tend to get exaggerated. It is understandable. Most of us get upset when we suddenly find ourselves disputing territory with a rattler or cottonmouth. My inclination is to give the snake all the room he wants—in fact, he can have the whole woods or swamp. I am not interested in shooting a snake, whether it's striking or sunning, until I have gained some distance and my nerves have unruffled a bit.

Another friend of mine consistently tells a snake story and swears to it. He was hunting bobwhite quail on a sunny afternoon and lagging behind his partner, who had already reached the pickup and loaded the dogs. My friend, with the pickup in sight, unloaded his 20-gauge, side-by-side double. He immediately stepped on an eastern diamondback rattler. The snake hummed angrily and drew back into an S to defend itself.

At least that's what my friend speculates the snake did. He was preoccupied with loading his shotgun while in mid-air. According to his story, when the snake buzzed, he jumped straight up so high that he had time to reload the double and shoot the snake before he came down.

He said, "I had to kill the snake before I landed because I jumped straight up and was coming down right on top of him."

The first time I heard the story, I asked, "Did you load one shell or two?"

My friend replied, "Why, I loaded two, of course! I was so nervous I might have missed with my first shot!"

I paused for a moment to calculate how high he would have had to jump in order to have had time to load two shells and shoot. I said, "You must have broken the world record for the high jump!"

"You would, too, if you stepped on a five-foot diamondback," he replied.

"How close to the snake were you when you finally shot?" I asked.

He said, "I had plenty of room. I fired at two paces, two long paces!"

Clothes Don't Make
the Hunter

Outdoor clothing has improved so much in recent years that it's now possible to look reasonably respectable while chasing a dog through the fields.

I do my shopping for outdoor accessories at local sporting goods or hardware stores. That way I see exactly what I'm buying, get to put my hands on it, and can take it back when it draws up or turns green. Also, it gives me a chance to catch up on the latest outdoor gossip, such as who is in trouble with his marriage for overstaying a hunting trip a month.

The mail-order houses do have the advantage of stocking unusual items that might not be found locally. If you go through the catalog pages, it's a dead cinch you'll come across an item you've urgently needed all your life, although you didn't know it existed until you went through the catalog. Not long ago, I was thumbing a catalog and found such an item, an egg peeler. The instant I saw a picture of it, I knew that I desperately needed it. My wife was not encouraging. She said if I bought it that I'd miss out on half my daily exercise.

I once ordered an outdoor casual shirt from a stylish company in New England. For 15 years, they had bombarded me with catalogs. Now that I've bought one item, I'll probably be receiving catalogs in my coffin.

The mail-order houses must swap mailing lists. It's a slow day when I don't receive five or six catalogs in the mail. The postal delivery man comes to my house to order his Christmas presents.

I study all the catalogs that arrive. I have never seen a catalog that didn't have pretty people modeling the clothes. There is only one conclusion: Only skinny young males hunt and fish; only gaunt females participate in outdoor affairs.

There are a lot of fat hunters, but they certainly can't buy their clothing by mail order. They are discriminated against, and so is anybody more than 30 years of age. Just once I'd like to see a fat model in a catalog. Also, I'd like to see a model who looked like he'd ever been hunting or fishing.

If you're a male and weigh more than 135 pounds, there's not much for you in the clothing catalogs. Not unless you could order live one of the skinny female models that weighs about 89 pounds.

I recently had a Western catalog of horsey clothing arrive unsolicited. Because I needed an anniversary present for my wife, I looked at the female shirt ads.

The models were uniformly pretty, in a tubercular way. Their clothing looked as if it had been painted on and then cinched up tight. The models gave the strong impression that the closest they'd ever been to a horse was a horsehair sofa.

Recently, a few of the hunting catalogs have been using male models with age. Elegant is the word for them. I'll bet it cost a lot to get all of those distinguished executives to pose in hunting clothes.

I bought one of their hunting coats last fall. My wife was disappointed in it. She said it didn't make me look skinny, younger, fashionable, or elegant.

She said I was the only hunter she knew who could make a new coat look wrinkled just by trying it on.

I had the coat on when I followed a brace of bird dogs through some recently burned palmettos and pine scrub. I got a total char job. My wife said she was glad to see me looking like my old seedy self.

The catalog models always seem to get their pictures made in city parks. Obviously, they just shaved and had pancake makeup applied to their faces and other exposed skin. The male models are the same. Even the dogs they pose with have every hair in its proper place.

The clothes fit so tightly they couldn't scratch their kneecaps. There's so little shoulder room they couldn't slap a mosquito without splitting something. There's no danger of them ever shooting anything, because they are bound so tightly they couldn't raise a shotgun or rifle. They do look good, though, in case they come across a formal cocktail party in the woods.

Personally, I'd like to take them hunting for a day in some greenbrier thicket and watch them climb through a few barbed-wire fences.

I'd donate the price of the most expensive item in the catalogs if I could take the models woodcock and grouse hunting for a day through some of the blowdowns in upper Michigan. It would be a good bet as to whether they first came bursting out all over in the knees or seat. In fact, as tightly as some of the stylish clothing is cut, it would make an interesting bet whether or not a model could actually cross over a blown-down hemlock.

Think of the fun you'd have taking the models through a moose bog, a duck flat, or chasing beagles in blackberry brambles. What about a hunt for Gambel's quail in the cactus country of Arizona? Just for fun, you'd wind up the day with a coon hunt at night in the mountains. Why, in one long day I think you could have the models looking like regular hunters.

The Packrats

Gun catalogs, shell boxes, wildlife calendars, and even the boxes guns are shipped in become valuable if you save them long enough. There's hardly a hunting or fishing item that some cult of collectors isn't scrambling after and willing to pay more than the original price.

The only catch is that you must have some place to store things such as old powder horns until the price soars. The nearer mint condition your antiques or rare items are, the more valuable they become. What the average sportsman needs for storage is something like an abandoned schoolhouse.

I have never enjoyed the luxury of having enough space to store such valuables as cartridge brass, old dog collars, and leaky johnboats. In fact, while our three children were growing up, the main thing I collected was a guilty conscience. I kept figuring if we ever got them through school and out of the nest, my wife and I would suddenly be rich and have unlimited space in our home.

It didn't work that way at all. The three kids are gone, but I don't have any more money now than I did when they were home. Poor dears, they must have been hardship cases during their years with us.

As each young adult left home, I rushed to claim the bedroom as storage for decoys, ice chests, and portable blinds. To my surprise, however, the kids didn't take anything with them. Every closet, desk, bureau drawer, and inch of wall space was filled with some belonging. In fact, two of the kids left their rooms padlocked!

It finally became clear that I had reared a family of packrats. The youngsters, of course, promised that their possessions were being left only temporarily and as soon as they settled into baronial palaces they would send for their goods.

It has been more than five years since the last one departed. So far, not one has sent for anything, unless you count money. They have, however, added to their inventory. From time to time, a United Parcel van arrives at our house with a huge carton from one of the kids marked, "For Storage." The cartons are also marked, "Collect."

Our attic rapidly filled with large boxes. In fact, I have difficulty weaving through the rafters to reach my old wooden cases that shotshells used to be shipped in. I like to check them to make sure termites are not feeding on them.

I also like to check on the stuffed heads that are wrapped in plastic. You know what happens if the wrapper is broken and certain beetles get inside.

It is probably possible to walk through our garage without stumbling over cartons sent by the kids for us to hold while they're getting relocated again. I say "probably possible" because no one has ever had the courage to try.

Somehow, it doesn't seem logical that three kids could leave home and I would end up with less storage space. I did manage to unload a few small items while my wife was on vacation, such as a motorcycle, jukebox, and tuba. That gave me enough space in the boy's room to store a few old guns I had bought at a sheriff's sale. I look on the pieces as valuable assets to leave my children. In the meantime, I'm sure they won't object if I use the guns during the hunting season.

We are basically so short of storage space that I keep many of my rods and guns under the beds. I have several map cases nailed to the ceiling in my room. It's awfully inconvenient! Besides that, our insurance only covered part of the cost of repairing my broken leg.

We are fortunate that the kids, plus one grandchild, always try to come home for Christmas and New Year's. We ask them not to bring any presents that can't be eaten or that are larger than a matchbox.

I don't know why my daughters get upset when they find a few hunting clothes hanging in their closets. I know some of the old steel traps might make them uneasy, but I always check to see that they are closed. One year, I stored a hunting coat and inadvertently left a dead quail in the game bag. This may have prejudiced the younger daughter when she opened the closet door a month later.

When the kids find something of mine in what used to be their rooms, they toss it into my cubby hole. I'm not sure by which particular squatters' rights they figure they own the rooms in perpetuity. My wife says it has something to do with eminent domain, like do I want to live here anymore.

I'm afraid to leave home during the holiday visits. A lot of my most decorative driftwood might be used in the fireplace. It was only last year that I came home to find the family laughing at one of my old hunting albums. I'm afraid to think what they were about to do with it!

This season, the kids have gotten together, pooled their money, and want to know what I'd like to have as a present. I told them something practical, like a warehouse with a row of bank vaults. Just once I'd like to get all my hunting and fishing gear lined up where I can find it without having to move dresses, hi-fi sets, sneakers, and bluejeans.

Deer Etiquette

There is a certain attraction to looking at dead deer. It is not a morbid appeal nor is there any gaiety attached. There is just mysterious fascination. There is no set ritual for looking at dead deer, but there are common patterns that develop from Panama to Alberta and from California to Virginia.

When driving down a highway, people cannot resist looking at wrecks, even trailers that have jackknifed and burned months before. This practice has a close kinship to standing and staring at dead deer. So has slamming on the car brakes to see a couple of garbage-can bears begging food from plump women in tight slacks on holiday in national parks.

When you take your kids on an educational vacation trip in the summer, they will not be impressed by scenic beauty, unusual geological structure, or the variety of forests. They may not remember much from a famous museum you take them through after suffering the hazards of driving in a strange city. If they can feed peanuts to some freeloading pigeons or squirrels, though, they will go into raptures.

If you pass a group of cars parked along a highway shoulder, with the passengers gathered below, your kids will insist on stopping. If some unfortunate deer has been terminated by an automobile, the crowd will stand gawking at the deer until an official truck arrives to move it. No one, including your kids, will leave until the truck disappears down the highway. The kids will remember that dead deer long after they have forgotten every educational feature you tried to show them, and when they can no longer recall which states they toured without checking the souvenir pennants on their walls.

Hunters are the same! After going on dawn patrol to catch peak whitetail movement around daylight, they hurry back to camp, eat breakfast, and then visit other camps to stare at dead deer. An hour or two before dusk, they may go back on stand.

A deer starer does not have narrow and specific requirements. Any dead deer will do. It can be a yearling doe, a forked buck, or an ancient shriveled buck without enough dental equipment to hurt a marshmallow. It is better, of course, if the dead deer has large size, unusual antlers, or some detail that makes it a little different from the run-of-the-mill whitetail.

If the dead buck has white splotches on the sides, it's worth an extra hour of staring and comment. A top prize for gazing is an all-white deer. If it's a true albino, with pink eyes, some of the starers will mill around and stare all night.

If you are driving down a back road and see a collection of pickup trucks, four-wheel-drives, campers, and old traps, with an assortment of hunters in a rough circle, you know they are staring at a dead deer, not necessarily a Boone and Crockett specimen, but just a plain old average six-point buck that collided with a bullet.

The etiquette of the situation is generous. Anyone, especially a hunter, has the right to stop his vehicle, get out, and join the crowd and stare at the dead deer. Not only that, he is welcome.

As he approaches the crowd, he will notice that the earlier arrivals have three basic physical positions for staring. A person who has been watching the dead deer for a long time will be leaning against a pickup truck with one hand in his pocket and the other hand propping up his head. He will be chewing on a piece of grass, a straw, a kitchen match, or tobacco.

The second group will be standing with shoulders slumped and both hands in their pockets, looking toward the ground and the deceased deer. They will occasionally rest their eyes by moving them to a spot on the ground, which they will begin excavating with light boot kicks. They'll kick dirt a bit, then stare at the dead deer some more, and then go back to kicking, but they'll seldom raise their eyes to horizontal level.

You can tell the native sons, those who are the local farmers, loggers, or lingering loafers at crossroad stores. They are squatters, their hands wrapped around their knees and their fannies touching their heels. You know they are country boys because no city man has legs strong enough to squat that way for long without toppling over or fainting.

The fellow who stands by himself, and the only one still holding a rifle, is the one who shot the deer. He is the one who does most of the talking. He may pace back and forth, but never far from the dead deer. No matter where he walks, he is given a certain amount of space. The others do not crowd in on him because he is the accepted leader of the congregation.

He does not stare at the ground, but holds his head high. He does not put a hand in a pocket because he needs it to explain the detailed history of how he came to shoot the deer. The free hand is for emphasis. The other hand grasps the rifle, and you hope it's unloaded.

The deer slayer adopts a certain air of modesty. He has killed the deer, but he wants you to know he is still one of the boys. He eagerly, but patiently, answers all questions. He will gladly show you the hole in the deer hide where the bullet entered and, if the bullet went all the way through, he will accommodate you by rolling the deer over and showing you the larger exit point.

As each vehicle arrives with a new crowd of deer starers, he will enthusiastically tell his success story over again with all the details such as bullet weight, caliber, and paces to the fallen deer. He will answer any questions you might have on ballistics or whitetail hunting in general.

If you are walking a dog on a leash in a large city, it is proper etiquette to open a conversation with any stranger, even one of the opposite sex, who also happens to be walking a dog. It is roughly the same in deer country. As a deer hunter, or outdoor lover of any kind, there is no breach of manners if you approach a man with a dead deer and stare at it for a while. You are entitled to ask any question you wish.

You may also take your forefinger and punch the upward ham as though you were a cattle buyer and knew how to test meat by feel. You can grasp the tail and wiggle it back and forth. You can also touch the antlers, but you should do this gently and with reverence. Naturally you do not make any movements that might suggest that you would damage as much as a hair on the hide.

You may stare at the deer for as long as the owner leaves it there. Although the deceased deer may be a runty spike, the etiquette of the situation demands that you say something complimentary about the buck. If you can't think of anything, then make a kind remark about the hunter's shooting ability or how good the venison should taste. After all, if he lets you stare at his deer, the least you can do is say something nice. Besides, some day you might be the center of attention as hunters crowd around to stare at the yearling buck you just shot!

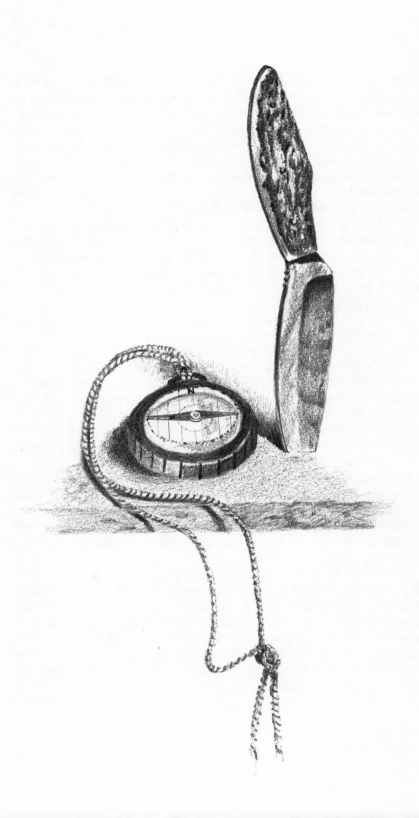

All He Wants for Christmas

Wives and other people connected with hunters seem to have trouble in selecting Christmas gifts for them. This is difficult to understand. I've never known a hunter who owned all the gear he thought he needed. Even if he owns it, the odds are that he can't find it.

A lot of my equipment is in an indefinite state. That is, I know I once bought it, but I can't locate it. I know it's in the garage, in the attic, under my bed, or around the house somewhere, provided I didn't lend it to another hunter or my wife didn't give it to the junk man.

When a hunter urgently needs a piece of equipment, he wants it right now. He's leaving on a trip in five minutes. It's of no value to remind him that he bought the equipment only last week and it has to be around someplace. If you can't find it, that's the same as not owning it.

When a hunter can't locate a piece of gear, the best thing for his wife to do is go to a movie across town. The situation is not improved by her hanging around and making remarks about how her mother taught *her* orderly habits. A lot of marriages have been broken by a wife saying, "There's a proper way to store each item and keep an accurate inventory."

Missing items are a clue for a Christmas present, if the marriage survives. The wife can give her husband a home computer. Correctly using a computer is a good way to keep track of outdoor gear, assuming the hunter can find the computer when he needs it.

Last Christmas I hinted around for a computer and once openly mentioned it to my wife. There was not a long discussion about it. She said, "For a man who can't figure out how to get a can of gun oil to spray, I don't think you're ready for programming a computer!"

Hunters always need replacement gear. A gift buyer need not worry about duplication. Even if the hunter already owns a dozen of the items, it's desirable to give him another. By the time he opens his gift on Christmas morning, he'll need it badly.

Years ago, I used to hunt California valley quail with a friend from his Jeep. It was usually hot, dry, and dusty. Carlos always remembered to take an ice chest full of bottled soft drinks but invariably forgot an opener. I used to hide openers in the Jeep, but we could never find them when we urgently needed a dust buster.

In all my weekly hunts with Carlos, we never forgot our guns, shells, dogs, or refreshments. Somehow, though, he never had a bottle opener when he needed one. I could eventually pop the bottle caps off against rounded ridges on the Jeep, but not without scraping a knuckle or barking skin.

When his wife, Rosa, asked me what she could buy him for Christmas, I went home and did some map work. The next day, I told her the best present she could give him was 114 cheap bottle openers. I would take them out between Christmas and New Year's Day and hang them from mesquite trees. The theory was that no matter where Carlos drove in his customary quail range, he would never be more than 100 yards from an opener.

It was a practical gift and worked for a while. When the next Christmas rolled around, he couldn't find most of the openers. Mesquite clumps changed, range cattle knocked a few openers down, and Carlos has a poor memory for openers.

When Rosa asked about Christmas gifts again, I suggested that she give her husband 114 wide swatches of fluorescent-orange cloth. This is sometimes known as "hunter orange" and is the most visible of all colors in varying light conditions.

Using my base map from the Christmas before, I would locate each bottle opener, replace missing ones, and tie an orange marker swatch high in each mesquite tree. The beacon would flutter with the wind and Carlos would never be out of sight of a bottle-opener location. He could hunt in peace and comfort. When the valley quail flushed, he could concentrate on his shooting, without distracting thoughts of how he would get the next bottle open.

Carlos was delighted with his present on Christmas morning, once Rosa explained how the swatches would be used. She is a loving wife and had cut and sewn reinforced buttonholes in each strip. A three-foot-long yellow string was tied through the hole to make it easy to hang the markers from mesquite trees. Carlos was quick to recognize the practicality of the gift. He joyfully exclaimed, "Even when we drive out after dark, we can see the flags and be able to refresh ourselves."

By the time Christmas approached the following season, most of the pennants were gone. The absentee landlord had visited his property and, thinking surveyors had been mapping for a railroad or highway, had torn the markers down. He might not be able to stop builders and eminent domain, but he could make things inconvenient.

He at least solved Rosa's problem of what to buy Carlos for Christmas that year. The day after Christmas, I was in quail territory with four gallons of orange paint making wide circles on mesquite trees. By fall, the marked trees had been mistakenly cut by an outfit making mesquite charcoal.

It went this way for several years until flip-top cans came out. I eagerly took a dozen to Carlos and told him his bottle-cap problems were over. He pulled one of the lifts. It snapped off. He tried another. It peeled off unevenly, leaving a needle hole. Carlos said, "As a matter of safety, perhaps Rosa can give me some can openers for Christmas? There are plenty of mesquite trees left."

I stared off into space. I was thinking how easy it is to select Christmas presents for hunters. They *always* need *sensible* items.

No Pain, No Game

Anybody taking one good look at Marcus Turnbull down in the Big Bend Country of Texas wouldn't dare call him a rhinestone cowboy. In fact, they wouldn't call him anything but "Mister," and they'd say that softly. Marcus, of course, wouldn't know what a rhinestone is, and if he saw one he'd call it a "play pretty."

Marcus is a real rawhider, there always being some part of his outer layer that's healing from a recent encounter with rock, bull, mesquite, or horse. There's not much of his original hide left without a scarred memorial to a dispute over space with a fence post or steer. Exposed skin, such as that on the back of his neck, is dry enough to soak up a gusher.

The first time I went hunting with Marcus for Texas whitetail deer high above Maravilla Canyon and Persimmon Gap, he developed a toothache in one of his back molars. Marcus doesn't talk much, doing most of his communicating with grunts and finger pointing, and once in a while breaking loose to say "yep" or "nope." If he's feeling real talkative after a supper of refried beans and bacon, he might say two words in a row, such as "Good grub."

The only way I knew something was bothering him the second day out was that I kept noticing tears streaming down his face. When we finally rested the horses and took a little breather on a rim at about 3,500 feet, Marcus walked off by himself as if scanning for whitetails. In that section of Texas, the Texas and Carmen subspecies of whitetail scrounge out a living high in the mountains and the mule deer take the lower foothills and arroyos. It's kind of backward from what you'd expect, but in the Big Bend Country you learn to live with a lot of strange things.

I was worried about Marcus. His camp was a day's ride from the nearest trail. The last mile or so, you don't ride the horses, but lead them as you pick your way along. Marcus doesn't care for other parties when he's hunting. I've been there several times since, but I still couldn't find my way back with a helicopter. We always enter and leave a different way. It's not like hunting Central Park, and if somebody has to get out of there you just can't rush it.

Marcus didn't waste time telling me he had a zinging tooth. He just pointed to his saddlebags and said "Pliers." When I got them, he spread his mouth open and said, "Pull!"

I took a quick look and could see that his lower jaw was swollen and probably infected. The last thing on earth I wanted to do was try and wiggle that molar out! I sat down on a hot rock and said, "Marcus, there's gotta be a better way of handling this. Let's talk about options."

He had a forefinger in each side of his jaws spreading his mouth to show me what I didn't want to look at. As far as I could understand, the longest oral message he had ever given at one stretch was, "Sumitch gotta cumout!" Then he pointed at his throbbing tooth with a forefinger, jabbing the finger back and forth, and finally pointing it at the pliers.

My medical experience is limited. I have cut a few porcupine quills from dogs, dug out fish hooks, and poured iodine on cuts. I once extracted 28 pieces of rock from the hind end of a trailbike rider who had failed to make a turn and traveled 40 feet down a gravel bank on his rump. On the other hand, I had never extracted a tooth even under the most favorable of conditions.

While I was searching my conscience, or more likely looking for an excuse, Marcus helped me make up my mind. I looked up to see a .45 revolver pointed at my midsection. It was a very clear communication. My options had run out.

Just like they do in the movies, I struck a match to sterilize the inside of the pliers. Marcus grunted, shook his head, and walked over to his saddlebags. He reached in and came out with a bottle of chili peppers, his own brand that he dries each fall and then probably mixes with Red Devil lye, cyanide, and blasting powder. He saturated the pliers with the germ killer and took a huge mouthful and squirted it around his gums. Whatever the results of the extraction, I knew we'd have no trouble from germs.

Marcus did not have complete faith in me. As he sat on a rock facing the sun, he kept the revolver pointed at my stomach while I gently probed. I wasn't quite sure which tooth had worn out its welcome. When I sensed that he had returned the revolver to its holster, I knew I had found the right one.

I tried to remember how dentists had removed my wisdom teeth, but I had always been so doped up that all I could recall were the little nurses holding my hands. I decided that pulling a tooth must be a little like shooting a rifle. I took several deep breaths, tried to relax, took a deep breath, and let half of it out. Then I squeezed the pliers firmly, wiggled them back and forth, and jerked! The pliers came out of his mouth and, miracle of miracles, there was a tooth with bloody roots.

Marcus stood up and spat. He opened the chili-pepper jar, took out a pepper, and put it as a poultice on the vacant gum. Then he pointed toward a distant slope and said, "Deer."

"Just a minute," I said. "Hold your hosses. We're going to give this tooth a proper burial." I kicked a hole in the dobie and carefully placed the tooth in the bottom and then covered it with the dry soil. I took out a pad and pencil and wrote a note. I dated it and put the note in a plastic device carried in most men's wallets. Then I gathered nearby stones and covered it with a four foot cairn.

Whenever I hunt in the Big Bend with Marcus, I insist that he take us by the marker for a nostalgic visit. We usually sit there for half an hour or so, each with his own thoughts. I have never asked him what he would have done with his revolver if I had refused to pull that tooth. Marcus has never asked me what I wrote in the note. It said, "Here lies a molar from Marcus Turnbull and five years of Charley Dickey's life. Rest in peace!"

Catch and Release

Some famous person once said that a gentleman is one who shows grace under pressure. A true sportsman is one who can catch a large fish, release it, and never tell anyone. He measures up to his own standards, and that's all of the satisfaction he needs.

By this definition, there are not many true sportsmen around. It's like having a solid gold Cadillac in the garage but never being permitted to drive it around the block to show it off. It hurts all over.

I have tried to be a true sportsman several times. Once or twice it has lasted as long as an hour. I was happy to release the fish, but I was busting to tell someone—anyone! In fact, I had to tell somebody or explode.

Last year, I fished a lake by myself, which was about a two-hour drive from home. Fishing conditions were ideal, and I caught a big bass, at least it was big compared to most bass I catch. She had given me a good battle, including three spectacular jumps, so I gently unhooked and released her.

I managed to load my boat on the trailer, say goodby to the fishermen and loafers hanging around the dock, and leave without mentioning my fabulous fish. An hour down the road, in a sparsely settled rural area, I was overwhelmed with a compulsion to tell another human being about that bass.

For a brief moment, my resolution came back. I said to myself, "How silly can you get? No one in the whole world really cares that you caught an eight-pound bass."

Another voice inside me whispered, "But they need to know!"

To ease the conflicting inner turmoil, I rolled down the driver's window and shouted to the world in general, "I caught an eight-pound bass. There was no luck involved. It was all skill!"

I yelled at hardwood and coniferous trees, fallow fields, and planted ones. I shouted over and over, but it didn't give me any relief. I saw a field of horses and pulled off on the shoulder, got out of the car, and hollered at them. I received no consolation, the horses only turned and bolted away.

A feeling of panic was taking me over. I had to tell another human being about that fish! I was like a four-pack cigarette smoker in his second hour of kicking his habit. Although I was not yet in a state of delirium, I was beginning to wonder if it was safe for me to drive.

Suddenly, across a quarter-section field, I saw a farmer on a tractor plowing parallel to the road. I slammed on the brakes, jumped out of the car, and began waving my arms. The farmer didn't see me and kept going. I considered running into the field to chase him down, but there was a high fence capped by three strands of barbed wire.

Then, I realized that when the farmer got to the end of the row he would turn. He'd see me then. So, I took my boots off and climbed on top of the car and waited. As the farmer made his turn and started back down the field, I waved frantically. I saw him slow, and knew he had seen me.

I figured he'd cut his engine off, I'd yell across the field, and that would do the trick. The farmer must have sensed my distress, however, because he headed my way.

As I paced up and down the car top, the farmer raced across the field. When he was about 20 yards from the fence, he turned the tractor, cut the engine, and sat waiting.

"Thank God you're here," I screamed. "You arrived just in the nick of time."

The farmer, a huge man in his middle 40's, jumped from the tractor cab and ran toward the fence. "What is it? Has somebody been hurt?"

"No," I replied, "it's nothing like that. It's good news!"

The farmer stared at me carefully and asked with a hopeful lilt, "Did Congress raise the subsidies?"

"Better than that," I said. "I caught an eight-pound bass."

"You what?"

"It's like this. I was bumping some structure with a worm over at the big reservoir and this bass . . . ."

"You did what?"

"Like I was saying, I was bumping a purple worm at 12 feet and suddenly I felt this tap-tap and . . . ."

The farmer bellied up against the fence, grabbed the wire, and glared at me. He slowly looked me over from head to foot and then back again.

Then he said in a grinding voice, "You called me all the way over here to tell me about a fish?"

"Sure, I thought you'd like to know about my bass," I replied.

When I saw his knuckles getting white and his face red, I knew that farmer was coming through the fence or over it, barbed wire and all. I realized that I urgently needed to be someplace else, and I jumped off the car. I slowed half a mile down the road and looked back. The farmer was still standing there squeezing the fence.

As I unpacked my gear at home, my wife asked if I had caught anything. I nonchalantly replied, "Oh, I caught a little old eight-pounder."

"Great," she smiled, "let's see it."

"Can't," I said, "I released the fish."

I hate to see my wife roll around on the ground like that. After she got her breath back from laughing, she whooped, "If you'd caught a bass that big you'd be all over town showing it off." Then, she ran into the house laughing hysterically, but not before screaming, "Threw it back my asterik!"

Deer Mathematics

Somebody is always coming up with something trying to make hunting a science rather than a matter of judgment or pure luck. Now the Wildlife Management Department of Virginia Polytechnic University has come out with a formula purported to be extremely accurate in assaying the weight of a deer in the field.

First, you have to kill the deer. This leaves out a lot of judgment and luck in the process, but we are talking about the weight-estimation process, and you must have something to estimate. With a simple tape measure, you can quickly determine the deer's weight where it lies. You simply multiply the deer's chest measurement (girth) at the heart by 5.6037 and then subtract 94.0982 from the result. This will give you the estimated live-weight of your deer.

The person who made this wonderful discovery obviously was not a deer hunter. He had never heard of the buck fever one gets on first spotting a buck which strolls into range. Or the shakes one gets when he reaches a large buck he has just downed. I use the word "large" in a relative sense. It may be a scrawny six-point buck dying of malnutrition, but if it is bigger than any other deer he has ever shot, to the lucky hunter the animal is a monster. When the realization hits the hunter that he has actually killed the buck, he may be stricken by anything from the shakes to a double case of Jake-leg. It is highly unpredictable what sort of trauma the deerslayer may experience.

The last thing I'm worried about is the weight of the deer, once I am assured the hunter's trophy is dead beyond recall. First, I try to get the hunter's rifle away from him. I have seen a new hunter, with his first trophy lying dead on granite outcrops, stand there and pump bullet after bullet into the dead animal, fearful that it might fly away. I am always reluctant to try and take someone's firearm when he is firing away.

I have seen experienced hunters arrive at a big dead buck and go into a wild Indian war dance, circling the animal and waving a loaded rifle in many directions, including mine.

On the few times I have caught lunker bass, such as those weighing at least two pounds, I have found it best to sit quietly and rest and think of peaceful things such as bonuses and cemeteries. That way, no one sees my hands shake while I am tying a new knot on the plug. It's the same with downed deer. I unload my gun, move it to a safe distance, sit on a log, and try to act calmly. I can do this with confidence because I know that any of my buddies who arrive will want to look over the deer. They'll want to push it a few times with their boots, the same way they kick tires when buying a secondhand car.

My buddies are not looking for my fresh bullet hole. What they hope to find is one three days old or older, preferably with a little green around it. Then, they can say I shot a buck which was on its last legs. They may go so far as to say that the buck was lying down, gasping its last breath, and I came along and shot it. In addition, they might make remarks about the buck having powder burns, as though I had shot it from 10 feet rather than pulling off a magnificent shot at 200 yards through brush.

By the time they get through making their kindly remarks, my hands are shaking no more than usual; that is, any finger has at least a 20-pound pull.

I am sure the biologists at VPU worked hard to come up with their formula. I wouldn't dream of knocking it. Who, though, after the excitement of shooting a buck, can remember numbers such as 5.6037 and subtracting 94.0982? I can't remember my wife's birthday, even after getting hints for 11 months.

One might suggest that the formula be written down and put in a hunter's wallet. That sounds reasonable, but I have put the date of my wife's birthday in my wallet several times, and I have never yet been able to find it. At least, I can never find it when it is needed most, just ahead of her birthday.

The VPU biologists did suggest that the key numbers could be reduced to C (for chest) x 5.6 minus 94, and that could be written on your hunting license. The plus or minus error is insignificant as compared with carrying decimals to Timbuktu. Even on a big buck, the theory goes, the short form would make only a few ounces of difference. Well, you can tell those biologists aren't bass fishermen.

I suppose a hunter could take a small card and put it under the butt plate of his rifle. Then, when he needed to weigh a buck, all he'd have to do would be take the butt plate off. This, of course, totally discounts the post-kill symptoms of buck fever mentioned earlier. I find it hard to visualize a thoroughly excited hunter being able to take off a butt plate.

The real point, however, is that deep down a hunter doesn't want to decide on a buck's weight until he uses a few formulas of his own. His best bet on estimation is when the buck is in the field, before it has moved. In red clay country, the buck may have a pound or so of clay on its feet. Clay is heavy, and to guess on the safe side, a buck might be hauling as much as four or five pounds. Because the clay is stuck between the hooves, it is a part of the deer and should be included in the total field-weight estimation.

Depending on where the buck was hit, he may have lost a lot of blood. Because blood has many minerals in it, it is heavy. A buck also has on the average 12.5 bowel movements a day—some biology student probably got a Ph.D. for that discovery. When a buck is hit with a bullet, it loses kidney fluid and bowel pellets. If the buck ran quite a piece before falling, he may have had more than one bowel movement. It's safe to say the deer lost weight this way.

No biologist yet has figured an exact formula for adding these losses. That doesn't mean a hunter, being an honest and observant person, shouldn't make his own best guess.

Suppose the buck, before being shot, was driven a considerable distance by dogs or hunters or both. The buck would have lost body moisture. Again, the hunter should add his best guess, such as maybe the buck had been running for about three days.

It might have been a dry summer and fall. The buck found little surface water and dew to drink or lap. The vegetation was not as moist as it should have been. With any luck at all in the rainfall, the buck would have been much heavier.

As bucks approach the rutting season, for at least 60 days in most latitudes of the U.S., they add fat, especially in the brisket. As they spar, though, with saplings and overhanging limbs, they lose a lot of weight. It's worse when they hit the peak of the rut and seldom sleep or eat, spending most of their time searching for receptive females.

A mature buck, one 3½ years or older, can lose 30 to 40 pounds or more chasing around during the rut. Perhaps you remember how it was when you were in high school and college?

No one ever shoots a buck before this fat loss occurs. This gives the hunter a chance to say, "If I'd shot him six weeks earlier, I bet he'd have weighed 25 pounds more. Look at how poor his brisket is!"

Later on, when you ask a hunter how much his buck weighed, he'll say 205 pounds. He's always talking about the full, on-the-hoof live-weight, including mud, blood, and pre-rut fat. He doesn't volunteer that this was live-weight or say anything about all the hair that was rubbed off dragging the deer out of the woods.

He'd prefer that you think the 205 pounds was field-dressed or hog-dressed weight. I have never understood the difference between the two, except that I know whichever one the hunter uses gives a weight advantage.

I once went deer hunting with a good friend in cotton country in Alabama. To protect the name of the guilty, I'll call him Preacher. He shot a big buck, one of the largest I had ever seen. I guessed that the buck, with teeth suggesting five years of age, weighed 250 pounds on the hoof. Preacher said the buck would weigh 275 pounds or there wasn't a boll weevil in Alabama.

We didn't field or hog dress the buck, but we about broke our backs getting the deer loaded onto the bed of a pickup truck. By the time we got to camp, there were five or six hunters loafing around. They didn't lose any time guessing how much the buck weighed, estimating from 210 to 300 pounds. Then the cook came out, walked around the pickup, and said, "Preacher, I been cooking deer all my life, and that there one will weigh 325 pounds if he weighs an ounce."

The old cook was a dandy fellow about 20 years past senility, and I figured his I.Q. had sunk to -10. He was smart enough to know, though, that the Preacher owned the camp and the land.

Because the countryside was filled with cotton gins having scales which would weigh well more than 500 pounds, I made the stupid suggestion that we take the deer and get an accurate weight. The Preacher gave me a hard look and said the buck weighed 325 pounds, and he knew as much as any scales. The old cook sidled over to me and whispered, "You better let that buck weigh 325 pounds if you ever 'spects to hunt back over here again."

That weight of 325 pounds still stands as a "record" for that section of Alabama. Any time I'm in that section at the crossroads stores, I swear I saw that big buck weighed on cotton-gin scales. Furthermore, anybody weighing under 100 pounds who wants to challenge it, I'll invite them outside for fisticuffs.

Some old bucks with pretty fair antlers don't necessarily have big bodies. Some bucks big in body have only fair racks. Theoretically, the first nutrition a deer eats goes to body growth and repairs. Secondarily, the nutrition left over goes to the antlers. Heredity gets a little mixed up in the process.

The thing is that once you get a good deer head mounted and hanging in your den, the buck on the hoof can weigh about any reasonable amount you want him to. Nobody can prove anything. Just be sure that right after you kill the buck, you don't tell your wife the true weight. She'll give you away every time anyone even glances at the head mount.

According to the VPU biologists, a deer's live-weight multiplied by .78 will give you his field-dressed weight. And about half the field-dressed weight of your deer will be meat for your freezer.

That's a nice thing to know, but I'm not sure how often the formula will be used by successful hunters. I grind up a lot of the venison I happen to acquire and make hamburger out of it with about 25 percent sausage, with a minimum of herbs. If I decide to give some of it away, such as to a man who owns a good bass pond, I make it easy for him to accept by saying, "Our freezers are chock-full of venison, and I'd be proud if you'd take a little off my hands." It's not pertinent to the situation that he know the live or dressed-weight of the deer the venison came from.

When a hunter stops by my house to offer me venison, I don't ask him the chest measurements of his buck. I know I'll have to listen to a long story about how he killed the monster at 600 yards, how he had tracked Old Slew-foot for two years, and why he was finally able to outwit the buck. After all of that, I'm not in a mental condition to work mathematical formulas. Besides that, if I catch him in a slight exaggeration, such as 100 pounds, I can't tell him. A man can lose some of his best friends that way.

Actually, most deer hunters are pretty honest. They're just about like bass fishermen. In fact, it has been my observation that most bass fishermen hunt deer and vice versa.

Fish Psychosis

One out of five to one out of three patients leaves an American hospital with a medical problem caused by the care given, according to a recent article syndicated by the *Washington Post*. Lowell S. Levin, Yale Medical School professor, was quoted as saying, "That is an epidemic by anyone's judgement."

Without getting into a squabble about the medical industry, I'd say the hospitals are doing pretty good. My own research indicates that of every five fishing trips made by the average angler, on at least four of them he comes home in worse condition than when he left.

My data shows that on 99.99 percent of the fishing trips the angler comes home with less money than when he left. Now that's an epidemic. Once in a while you can cut your losses on hospital stays by having medical insurance. As a rule, though, your policy doesn't cover the part you had repaired, removed, or replaced.

There's no policy on fishing to spread your financial disasters. They are flat losses not accepted by your wife, credit union, or the IRS. The only reason that .01 percent of the anglers do not lose money is that the car won't start and they never get out of the driveway.

Fishing is supposed to be relaxing. The fishing industry touts it as therapeutic. Philosophers write sentimental wisdom about fishing, such as those days spent on a stream are not deducted from your allotted time on earth. Even some psychologists go fishing on weekends so they can gather strength to face patients the following Monday. Who are they trying to kid? What's relaxing about launching your boat with the plug left out? And, at a public dock where there are a lot of loafers and all of them laughing hysterically as your boat sinks?

My research on fishing clearly shows that any regular angler is likely to acquire a psychosis of some sort. A psychosis is any severe mental disorder, with or without organic damage, characterized by deterioration of normal intellectual and social functioning and by partial or complete withdrawal from reality.

A typical psychosis is when you have cast for eight hours without getting a strike but think that if you cast one more time a monster fish will hit. Anglers refer to this phenomenon as optimism. Psychiatrists refer to it as a withdrawal from reality, or a budding psychosis.

If the angler casts from dawn until dusk for two days without a strike, he calls it persistence. Where, however, is the relaxation and peace of mind? If he insists on fishing the second night, before returning home, he is well into psychosis, with or without organic damage.

Deep down there is bound to be emotional damage. The angler, with his computer brain and scientific equipment, has been badly whipped by a fish with a primitive brain no larger than a pea. The fisherman's pride suffers, and there is a loss of self-esteem. He blames it all on the weather, another withdrawal from reality. He goes home with feelings of guilt, something he did not have before he went fishing.

When he arrives home, his wife cheerfully meets him in the driveway and brightly asks, "What'd you catch, honey?" For that particular moment she has the wrong attitude. She should be wearing sackcloth and ashes, not a cheery disposition.

He replies in one of three ways. He loses his temper and shouts, "Not a blankety-blank thing!" Or, he answers sarcastically, "I caught a cold." Or, he may grunt or mumble something which indicates he wants to hide from normal social functioning and pout awhile.

There is no limit to the types of psychosis an angler can develop over the weekend. Suppose that his fishing buddy has outlandish luck while he is going fishless. He may withdraw from reality so completely that he is physically unable to see his companion's fish. He experiences a blackout and may exhibit antisocial behavior until some future fishing trip when he catches the most and largest fish. When this happens, he experiences a profound personality change. He leaps from the swamp of depression to the heights of exuberance.

There are other things an angler can bring home which he did not have when he departed. These include: sunburn, windburn, new freckles, mosquito bites, and an extra pound or two from comsuming too many refreshments. He may come home with a hook in his shoulder, which requires a trip to the hospital emergency room, which his insurance policy does not cover. He may even return late at night with a few fish which he insists on cleaning in the kitchen his wife has spent all weekend cleaning.

There are a great number of things he had when he departed that he might no longer own when he returns. For instance, he may have forgotten to hook the safety chains when he attached the boat trailer to his car. The boat may now lie in eternal peace at the bottom of a rocky cliff. If he was lucky, he did not drop his glasses or camera overboard while fishing. He may have lost an anchor, left his favorite rod at the dock, and knocked a blade off the propeller.

He does not consider the loss of plugs, plastic worms, spoons, and spinners. These are a normal expenditure for any fishing trip, a built-in cost. If he took his family for a weekend of pleasure, he might discover as he arrives home that one of the children is missing and was last seen going to the restroom at a service station.

The angler is relaxed when he goes to work on Monday morning. He is grateful that he has five days to rest up before he has to go fishing again. He can lead a normal life until quitting time on Friday afternoon, or maybe even Saturday morning. He has time to get rid of his budding psychosis on the job before the weekend stresses start again.

The Art Collector

Hobart Sosebee, my neighbor and outdoor buddy, isn't exactly irresponsible about money. He just doesn't know how to handle it, unless you count handing it out.

Hobart looks at things differently than most people. For instance, it is typical of Hobart to buy a new shotgun on payday and not have enough money left for luxuries such as rent, food, and water. The path to Hobart's door is a network of runways trampled by utility people turning off meters and dunning agents trying to squeeze a turnip.

His wife, Flora, thought that because he already had 14 or 15 shotguns it was more important to pay the rent. Hobart's line of logic, however, was that the shotgun was on sale, guns are increasing in value, and it's a hedge against inflation. Besides, Hobart didn't own a pump with a modified choke.

Things have gone on a long time like that between Hobart and Flora. He once bought out all the reloading equipment of a sporting-goods store going out of business. He bought enough wads and shot to support a fair-size army, but all the hulls were 28-gauge, and he didn't own a 28 gauge shotgun. Technicalities don't bother Hobart. The next payday he bought a

Remington 1100 in 28-gauge and almost got evicted for nonpayment of rent.

Flora finally went to see his boss and made arrangements to have his paycheck mailed directly to her. Hobart was considerably upset about that, and you could hear them shouting at each other up and down the street. Flora kept saying that if he needed pocket change he could reload some 28-gauge shells and peddle them.

After Hobart's purchasing power was severly cut, the Sosebees began to catch up with the bills and even got a little ahead. Flora called me over one day and said, "Hobart needs a new suit. If he were to kick off, he doesn't even have a decent one to be laid out in. I don't want to embarrass him by taking him shopping. So, I'm giving you this $150 to take him downtown and get him a suit. Just don't let him get his hands on the money."

Well, Flora sure squeezed me in the middle. It was worse than two bird-dog owners asking me who had the best dog. Hobart said it was indecent of Flora not to trust him to buy a suit. When he found out I had $150, he brightened up and said, "We can get a good suit for $50. That'll leave us $100 to stop by Easy Joe's and pick up a secondhand rifle or maybe a scope."

"Hobart," I said, "how long has it been since you bought a suit? Fifty bucks will hardly get you one leg of a pair of britches."

On the way to town, Hobart casually mentioned that the Talbott house was having a sale of all furnishings. Old man Talbott had been a traveler and sportsman in his day, and before I knew what was happening, we were at the auction.

Hobart went rummaging around and checking the items still for sale. He was all excited when he came back to where I was sitting and said he had found an original Audubon painting. I told him that it didn't matter what he had found. He didn't have the money to bid on it.

He replied, "We can make a killing on that painting. It's worth thousands if nobody here knows it's an original."

He finally talked me into going back to look at the painting. It was part of a huge clutter. A section of the frame had been broken, and it looked as though the painting had hung over a fireplace. Hobart said, "We can get it cleaned up by an art student for next to nothing."

He slyly pointed to the artist's signature when no one was looking and said, "Now don't act excited like you've found something valuable."

I peered at the signature and read, "John James Au . . . ." The last letters were smudged over.

"Hobart," I said, "that dirty old painting doesn't look like any of Audubon's stuff I've ever seen. The turkeys look too natural and aren't straining their necks."

"You never did know anything about art," Hobart said. "It's the real thing. It's been hiding up here in this old mansion for no telling how long."

Anyway, Hobart talked me into letting him bid some of his suit money. I told him he could spend any amount up to $50. When the painting came up. Hobart bid $50 before the auctioneer even got started.

No one else said a word, and Hobart had bought a painting.

I was trying to get him out of there, but the auctioneer brought out some hand-painted decoys. Hobart said to me in a loud whisper, "We just made several thousand dollars. How about letting me use a little more of that suit money?"

Well, there were some old ladies that wanted the decoys to make lamps out of, and Hobart had to bid $100 to get four of them. Then, he hit me for an advance on his Audubon painting profit and bought a dozen 1920 calendars, some rat-chewed outdoor books, a U.S. Army canteen from World War I, and a pair of puttees for walking through wetlands.

He drained every cent I had buying old lanterns, kitchen knives, a rusty bayonet, and all sorts of things with hidden values that only Hobart could see. He kept telling me we'd make a fortune reselling the items to collectors.

On the way out, we ran into the art teacher from the high school. He looked at Hobart's prize painting and said, "Oh, you bought the John James Aubracken turkey painting. Crazy old coot used to live around here. The painting is worthless, but that broken frame might bring a few dollars."

Well, I'm on Flora's list now, right up at the top with Hobart. She's told it all over town that I don't have enough sense to go to town and buy a suit of clothes. At least she knows I'll look after Hobart. I don't want him kicking off until he pays me back and gets a decent suit to be laid out in.

There's Always a Way

One of the laws of nature is that everything is in a constant state of change. Given enough time, the things we look on as permanent will change. Sea level changes as ice caps melt, mountains are thrust up slowly from the ocean floor as other mountains are cut away, and even continents shift around and disappear.

Man is forever seeking solid permanence. It gives him a sense of stability and security. He measures time by his own life span because that is what is real to him. He is continually frustrated because his longing for permanence is thwarted by change. As he grows older, the changes seem to come faster and faster.

The hunter sees rapid physical changes, which he understands but finds hard to accept. Almost overnight he sees a favorite grouse covert changed into a subdivision. A small marsh, once considered wasteland except by sportsmen, no longer has room for ducks and shorebirds because it is covered with warehouses.

Perhaps even worse is that the hunter sees his old companions changing. The friend who used to hunt all day is now worn out in two hours. Some companions move away, and others depart down an unknown trail into eternity. The old buddies whom one counted on for so many years are not the same or are no longer there. There was only a temporary permanence.

Last fall, I received a letter from Petie Stover, a boyhood hunting pal, who had left town after graduating from high school and hadn't been back in all that time. Every four or five years, I'd receive a Christmas card from Petie, but never with any information. I figured he must have made a lot of money or been successful in some way to come back now, but his letter said that he simply wanted to walk one more time through the squirrel woods and rabbit fields we had hunted long ago. He also hoped to visit with any classmates who were still around.

I wrote Petie to come back and I'd show him around. I didn't tell him that our old squirrel woods were now industrial parks and the rabbit fields were covered in houses. There were still plenty of squirrels and rabbits, perhaps more than when we hunted as boys. They had adapted to the changed habitat and were thriving on suburban life.

When Petie arrived, I couldn't believe the changes in him. All of my memories were of a slender high school lad with sparkling blue eyes and a shock of rebel hair, each shaft reaching in an independent direction. The bright twinkle was still in his eyes, but he supported a budding paunch and the hair had thinned down to bare scalp. There were also arroyos in his cheeks and forehead that were hard to reconcile with the smooth face of long ago.

We spent the evening trying to catch up on the years that had separated us and what our old classmates were doing. It was easy for me to understand that Petie owned a chain of motels, but hard to accept that he was a grandfather. He was eager to go hunting the next morning so we stopped by a sporting-goods store for him to buy a nonresident license. Petie remarked that this was a big change. In the old days, the only place you could buy a license was at the courthouse.

The first place Petie wanted to go was the Widow Kopp's woodlot, a favorite place for hunting squirrels. I didn't have the heart to tell him about the change and simply drove him there and let him see the sprawling industrial park. If there was a tree or landmark left from our boyhood days, we could not find it. There were plenty of squirrels, and they boldly scampered across the lawns and roads fully protected except from roving dogs and automobiles.

Petie didn't say much as I drove him toward Sunny Dale, a subdivision now covering the broom sedge fields and hedgerows where we used to jump rabbits. It was easier to let Petie see it than for me to try and explain the changes.

It was the same at the Beech Farm, now overlain with an elementary school and its huge playgrounds. Graham's Bottoms, where we had flushed snipe and woodcock while hunting rabbits, was now refurbished with a box factory. I drove up to a knoll where there used to be an old apple orchard. It was always a good place to get a view of the town and surrounding area. Where we had once hunted rabbits and taken shots at grouse, the land was now occupied by the Everlasting Memorial Cemetery.

Petie insisted on getting out and walking around. Although it was well into the day, there were several cottontails hopping around the perimeter of the cemetery feeding on the lush vegetation. Petie sat down, plucked a stem of grass to chew on, and silently looked toward the expanding city below. He was really staring into time, though, trying to catch up with the changes.

Finally, he turned toward me and said wistfully, "I guess we could go down to the city dump and shoot rats."

"Not anymore," I replied. "our old dump is covered and there's an office building on it. The new dumps are kept sanitary and are filled in every day by bulldozers."

Petie didn't reply. He just kept staring off into space. After a while he said, "It's happening in my state, too, but somehow I thought things would always stay the same back home." There was a long pause as he fought with himself to accept the changes. Then he said, "If you haven't changed too much, you've got some place to hunt. Let's go there."

We drove 35 miles to the Big Sandy River, a distance we would never have dreamed of traveling in our boyhood just to hunt rabbits or squirrels. Although there was a project to straighten the river, the bottoms still had plenty of hardwoods and a good population of squirrels. Some of the old oxbows had swampy areas with the right habitat for marsh rabbits around the edges. After four hours of walking, sitting, and sloshing, we had about all the hunting our legs would tolerate.

We drove toward home with three grey squirrels and one dark brown rabbit. About halfway home, Petie said, "Those squirrels seem wilder than they used to be. And the swamp rabbits are a lot faster."

As we approached the city limits, he said, "Adaptation! That's the key. Do you realize we saw more squirrels and rabbits in town than we did in the river bottom? There's probably more game in the bottoms, but it's wilder and spookier. The town game is bolder because it's not bothered. Both have adapted to their conditions. Wildlife that doesn't adapt just can't make it."

Petie gave a long sigh. "Hunters can learn a lot from wildlife. Game has to accept change and adapt to it. So do hunters. The hunter who adapts to change will always find a place to hunt. The ones who don't, well. . . ."

Midnight's Cowboy

Riding horses are popular in the South, even for certain types of hunting. My personal opinion of horses is that they are not as good as U.S. choice beef.

Recently, a friend invited me to hunt bobwhite quail with him via horse transportation. At least, I had always considered him a friend until that moment. I asked him if he hadn't heard of a new contrivance for field transportation called an internal combustion engine.

He explained that there was no style at all in hunting from a pickup truck or Jeep. Anybody could do it without previous experience.

I asked, "Why be stylish?" Who was going to see us? We certainly weren't going to hunt birds down a main highway.

It is, however, a firm principle of mine to go along with the wishes of the man who owns the land and the quail. If he had said we were to fly from one covey point to another in a two-seat Messerschmitt, I would have shown up with aviator glasses. As it turned out, what he wanted was someone to toughen up his horse's back.

The cheapest way to toughen a horse's back is to invite an overweight rider to try and stay on his back between points. It's better if the rider is inexperienced and slides around a lot and toughens new areas. Horses do not uniformly love having their backs massaged this way.

On receiving the generous invitation, I immediately went down to Jake's Pool Emporium. It is the intellectual and social center of our village. A great many experts in varied fields hang around the Emporium. If you want to know how to run a government, program a computer, or how to empty a bar in a hurry, someone will know.

The main question I wanted to ask Jake was if horses are carnivorous. He assured me that all horses are vegetarians. I felt considerably better. I knew that if a horse had ever eaten a rider, somebody at Jake's would have heard about it.

Jake did say that some horses are full of fun and like to take a playful nip at a handy arm. One of the philosophers recalled a horse that had been fond of human ears; in fact, the horse found them irresistible and would lunge great distances for a chance at one. A second philosopher allowed that all horses had a secret desire to become place kickers.

From the information disseminated at Jake's, I gathered that it was reasonably safe to associate with a horse as long as you stayed in its middle. If you never let yourself be caught at either end, you might come home unmutilated.

That made sense. It's about the same with cars. If you keep a good position relative to the middle, even a skilled driver has a hard time hitting you crossing an intersection.

When I arrived for the hunt, my friend introduced me to the steed I was supposed to balance on all day. His name was Satan's Midnight Terror. I asked why his eyes were so fiery and bloodshot. My friend explained that was friendship reaching out.

As someone at Jake's had suggested, I brought several sugar cubes for my horse to assure him that all my motives were peaceful. When I handed Satan the cubes, I was quick and got nearly all my fingers back.

I asked if there was any particular reason my horse was named Satan's Midnight Terror. Did it, for instance, have anything to do with his habits or relationships with people? Did his name reflect his attitude in general toward life, especially that of a strange rider?

My friend smiled and said the horse was trained by a six-year old girl with a gentle disposition. If that was true, I asked, why did the monster have cuff marks all over his hooves and scars around his head? Why did he lick his chops when he looked at me?

I noticed that Satan was fitted with an English saddle, one of those skinny kinds without a horn to hold onto. My friend explained that it wasn't stylish to hold on to something while you were riding.

I said I wouldn't tell anybody if he wouldn't. Besides, the saddles of John

Wayne, Roy Rogers, and Gene Autry always had horns. That's what they held onto when the camera wasn't on them.

I don't know how high Satan was in hands, but he was about 16 feet at where there should have been a saddle horn. He was proportionally as wide. My friend pulled a pickup truck alongside Satan, and I crawled on the cab and then eased onto the horse.

It's awful hard to sneak on a horse without him knowing you're there. It was immediately apparent that my skeleton was not adequately flexible for riding astride. My exercise bicycle had not prepared me for such a wide beam. The only thing I could see to hold onto was Satan's mane, and I was afraid he would interpret this as too intimate a gesture.

When the dogs made their first point, I bailed out of the saddle yelling, "Geronimo!" I didn't shoot well all morning. I was soon exhausted from dragging Satan from point to point. That 1,500 pounds was the most excess gear I ever took on a quail hunt.

The Good Ol' Boys

Last fall I was warming my toes in the glow of oak embers at a hunting camp down in Chickasaw County, Mississippi. The supper dishes were as clean as we were likely to get them, and the conversation was low and easy. The hunters talked of huge bucks they had almost shot and other typical subjects when bellies are full and camp chores are done.

I listened intently because the dialect was strange and it was easy to miss phrases. The name of a deceased hunter came up and three or four funny stories were told about him. As the only foreigner present, I was reluctant to enter the conversation.

Finally, one of the hunters said, "Ol' John was a good ol' boy. A real good ol' boy." One by one, each hunter said the same thing. It was the highest praise they could give their departed friend. The last to speak was a dried-up hunter named Shadroe. If he had said a word during the two days we had been at camp, I hadn't heard it.

Shadroe looked at the floor, kind of like he was boring a hole in it, and said softly, "Yessir, ol' John was a real good ol' boy!" There was no need to say more about ol' John. The camp was quiet for a couple of minutes, as though each was paying silent thanks for having had the pleasure of knowing ol' John.

[173]

I broke the reverie by asking, "What's the definition of a good ol' boy? The term has been kicked around so much the past few years it seems to have lost definite meaning."

The last one I expected to answer was Shad. He jumped to his feet and started pacing the cabin. I won't try to use dialect because I'd get it wrong, but here's what he said, the best I remember.

Basically, a good ol' boy knows he's got all he can handle to run his own life and he doesn't try to run anybody else's. He's the finest example of the human race. He's a social animal and runs with a pack, group, community, or units of people wherever he happens to be. He puts loyalty to his herd above nearly everything else, but without losing his individuality. A rogue elephant can't be "a good ol' elephant" because he runs outside the herd. It's the same with a person. If he puts his own self-interest first, he'll never be a good ol' boy, no matter how much he craves it.

All politicians want to be good ol' boys, but not many ever make it. They're too self-centered, and when they try to act like one of the boys, their dishonesty and insincerity always show through. They might get elected as the lesser of two evils, but they don't fool anyone, and being elected doesn't qualify them as good ol' boys.

You can't campaign for election to the status of good ol' boy. The harder you work for it, the more it will elude you. Being a good ol' boy is a by-product of right living with your fellow man for the right reasons.

If a politician comes to a deer camp, he's got enough sense to make a big show of doing his part of the work. He doesn't have enough sense, though, to know he's doing it for the wrong reason. He wants to take credit for doing his part and impress everybody. He doesn't really want to do part of the work because he's helping other people. What he wants most is to be the center of attention.

When a good ol' boy arrives at camp, he pitches in to do more than his share of the work because it's for the good of the group. He doesn't expect or want credit or glory. He may go to camp two days early to chop wood and get everything ready for the others. They'll thank him alright, and he's human enough to like the appreciation. He doesn't chop wood for thanks, though. He does it to help the others!

You can't run for the office of good ol' boy because everybody can see through your motives. If you quietly go about doing things for people because you want to help them, however, some day you may qualify.

The people who award you with the honor of being a good ol' boy are usually the ones who know you best. They might not say much, but don't think you ever kid them. They know how loyal, honest, sincere, and kind you really are.

Nobody is in a hurry to elevate you to the status of good ol' boy. You have to prove yourself. One man might accept you as a good ol' boy in a week, but the next might hold up for 10 or 20 years. He wants to see how you do on the long haul.

A good ol' boy maintains his character and personality whether he's associating with people of greater or lesser money, education, or social status. He doesn't really care what color your skin is, who your grandpappy was, or what church you go to or if you don't go to any. He gives people the benefit of the doubt; that is, they ain't sonsuvbitches until they prove it.

If everyone wants to have a barbecue, but he hates barbecues, he'll volunteer to stay up all night cooking the pigs, goats, and venison. If he's at a dove shoot and some of the hunters don't stop at the limit, he figures that's their problem. They have to live with themselves. He won't lecture them, but when he gets his limit he'll stop.

On a hot quail hunt, a good ol' boy will water his dogs before he takes a drink. If the hunting vehicle breaks down, he'll tell you to keep hunting while he walks back to town to get a spare part. If he's taking more birds than you are, he'll be encouraging. If you're hitting more quail than he is, he'll compliment you on your shooting.

A good ol' boy is several shades higher than a gentleman. A gentleman can get a running start if he's born to wealth, position, or a cultured family. Inside he can be the biggest no-account in the country, but pretty well get away with being thought a gentleman. Maybe a few close acquaintances know, but that doesn't bother the "gentleman."

A good ol' boy has to earn every ounce of his title. What counts is what people know is inside him as reflected in the way he gets along with people and what he tries to do for them.

There ain't never enough good ol' boys. It's a Southern term, but I'm glad it's turning into a national term. There's nothing geographical about it. There's just as many good ol' boys in the North, Midwest, or West as the South.

I thanked Shad for his explanation. Then I thought I'd better go outside and get an armload of wood for the fireplace, plus enough to get the fire started first thing in the morning.

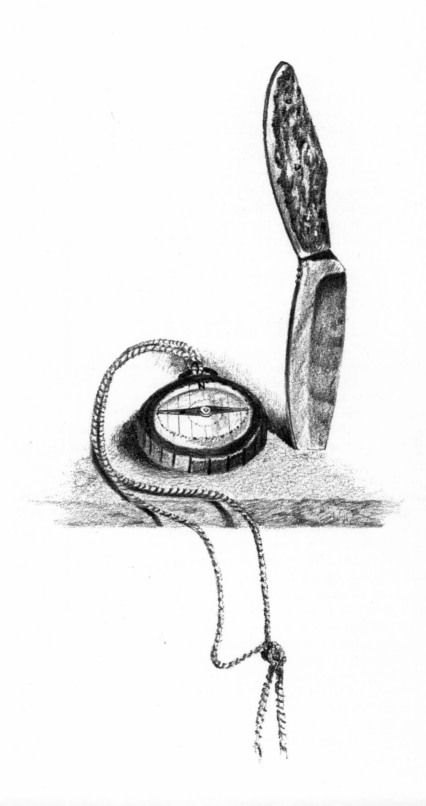

The Sport of
Disorienteering

Hikers traveling out of sight of their cars should always carry a safety kit in case they get lost. The kits should be put together with careful planning. After you get lost, it will give you comfort to remember what a great kit you left at home or in the car trunk.

According to survival experts, the simplest kit is a knife, waterproof matches, and a compass. I would also suggest a recent road map. It helps if you remember where you parked your car.

You should not feel embarrassed about getting lost. It happens to the best hunters, fishermen, and campers. Getting lost doesn't matter so much—it's getting found that counts! Don't try to get too technical about details. It doesn't matter if you find somebody or somebody finds you.

I once got lost in a blinding snowstorm, but I stayed calm and survived. On a return flight from Florida to LaGuardia Airport, I arrived in New York during the second night of an ice storm followed by windy snow. When I finally reached the long-term parking lot, dragging two heavy suitcases, I could not remember where I had left my car. An old ticket stub was of little help, saying only, "It's not safe to park a car anywhere in New York State."

I began trudging up and down the long rows of cars searching for mine.

Then, I noticed that all the cars were the same color—glazed ice. The paint, licenses, windshields, and frames were coated with several inches of ice. The parking lot looked like a tract development of igloos.

As the whirling snow increased, the visibility disappeared, and I suddenly realized that I was lost. Not only that, I was dressed in Florida clothing and my suitcases had frozen tightly locked. I paused to calmly review the situation, my survival kit being of little value in the lost car. I made a firm decision to get the heck out of there!

During a brief lull in the wind, I thought I heard loud voices arguing. That's where experience paid off. I knew it had to be New York taxicab drivers. I fought my way through the storm and found several drivers in a construction shed clustered around a barrel with a fire inside.

A cabbie looked at me, threw a racing form into the fire, and said, "Nanook of the North comes out of the storm!"

I was not too proud to ask for help in finding my car. First, I had the cabby take me to the nearest motel. Then I holed up for three days until the weather warmed. Finally I remembered that it was in Phoenix where I had left my car.

To this day, I have never forgotten that lesson. Before hiking a trail to a secret pond, I always write a note to myself saying something such as, "Car left by granite boulder at Stinking Creek Bridge." Then I fold the note inside my fishing license and put them both in my wallet.

It's critical to date the note. Wallets have a habit of becoming garbage dumps, and the first thing you know there are a dozen notes to yourself about where you've left your car. Without a date on your note, you can end up returning to your car in the wrong state. There is much to be said for survival kits but if we plan carefully we might never need them.

Not long ago, I wrote about some of the options you have when you find yourself lost. You can panic, you can try sincere praying, or you can call your mother. One of the tricks I've learned is to take your knife and cut a big piece of bark from a birch tree, or some other tree with flexible bark. You make a huge megaphone from the bark and then when you call your mother you can get more distance.

P. G. Hataway, a Louisiana pen pal, wrote a letter after reading of my options. He has developed the simplest and surest of safety kits to use when you get lost. It's a deck of playing cards. The cards are light, compact, and can be carried in a shirt pocket. Ideally, they would be waterproof.

When you get yourself irretrievably lost, find a flat place on the ground out of the wind. Sit down, take out the cards, and start a game of solitaire. It won't be long before someone is looking over your shoulder and telling you how to play the next card. Turn the unfinished game over to her, but not until she gives you directions out of the woods.

It is understandable how even an experienced outdoorsman can get lost in big swamps or vast mountains. This is especially true on overcast or foggy days. The indoorsman, though, doesn't understand how a fisherman can get lost on a lake. After all, the boat is trapped within the confines of the water and can't cross dry land.

Actually, fishermen seldom use the term "lost." They get "turned around" or "temporarily lose their bearings." They like "to explore new water" and "fish different areas." Their favorite landmark, a crow sitting in a tree, has "momentarily departed."

Fishermen know from bitter experience that they can get turned around on strange lakes, but they don't like to admit it. For some reason, it embarrasses them. It doesn't embarrass an angler driving down a highway to stop and ask for directions to Slim's Tackle Shop. But he'll circle his boat for hours before he gets up the nerve to ask a passing fisherman the location of Lunker Boat Ramp.

If you think anglers don't have secret fears of getting lost, watch them load a two-man boat before departing for half-a-day's fishing. There's not much room for walking after they load a case of soft drinks, an ice chest filled with sandwich makings, a crate of canned goods, and several brown bags. They hardly need that many refreshments for four hours of fishing. No matter how they try to disguise it, it's their survival warehouse for when they get lost.

The Old Equalizers

Dove shooting, according to one school of thought, is only a matter of physics. Two groups of matter cannot occupy the same space at the same time. So, the hunter fires his shot pattern so that a portion of it displaces the exact space a dove is attempting to temporarily occupy.

It's simply a matter of getting your shot exactly on time. Those who hunt mourning doves soon find that there are a lot of spaces above millet fields that are not occupied by doves, at least not when their shot passes through. The birds don't approve of the game and complicate it by flying in zigzags rather than straight lines. Doves also swerve, zip downward, zoom upward, and change speeds.

These aerobatics should not deter the hunter. They only make the game more challenging. No matter how the dove maneuvers, there is a mathematical formula that covers it. Any fourth-grade kid who has been through integral calculus and quantum mechanics can quickly work out the problem.

Actually, most shots are simple trigonometry. You estimate the speed and altitude of an approaching bird; you decide at what distance you will have your shot collide with it; and, you just have an easy problem in triangulation.

There are a few additional factors to crank in. For instance, from the time your brain decides to shoot until it can send out orders and actuate the component parts of your body, there is a lag time of about three-eighths to five-eighths of a second. This varies with each hunter, and you have to work out your own lag time. Science can't do it all.

There is also another variable. You know the muzzle velocity of the particular shot you are using. But the pellets begin to lose energy and slow the instant they leave the muzzle. The farther the pellets travel, the more they slow. For instance, it takes the same amount of time for the pellets to travel from 40 to 60 yards as from the muzzle to 40 yards.

These factors should not dismay the gunner. He simply cranks these variables into his equation. Basically, we're only dealing with one problem—making five or six pellets in the pattern occupy the same space as the dove at the same time.

We must estimate the speed of the dove. If the bird is flying level, our estimation is made easier. We also have to take into consideration variables such as tailwinds, headwinds, crosswinds, and gusts. If the bird suddenly swerves upward, we know it'll lose ground speed. If the dove dives, he quickly accelerates. We must consider these variables in our final equation.

Common sense tells us that if we shoot directly at a dove flying 45 mph our shot string will go behind the dove. We, therefore, must calculate a lead. The pellets must be fired ahead so that the dove collides with them. This lead is sometimes called deflection. The least lead you can get is zero, such as when a bird is flying straight away from you. The most lead you can get is 90 degrees of deflection, for example when the bird is flying in a path perpendicular to the position of your shotgun when fired. Of course, the deflection can be anywhere between 0 and 90 degrees, but at least you have these limits for your knowns. As with the other factors, the lead is simply made a part of your mathematical equation.

A dove flying at 45 mph ground speed covers 66 feet in one second. This means you have plenty of time to make all the necessary computations between the time the bird flies into range and then out, varying from two to four seconds from when you first spot your quarry.

One of the ways to make your mental computations quicker is to memorize certain knowns, such as a dove flying at an estimated speed of 45 mph is covering 66 feet per second. Of course, you don't want to get your sines and cosines mixed at a critical moment.

In any problem that is mathematical, I think it helps to break the components down so that one can more readily understand the final equation. If accurate knowns are cranked into the equation in the field, then the equation has to work.

The advent of inexpensive pocket computers has raised an ethical question about their use. Is it really fair to use a computer to work out a shooting problem on an approaching dove, or should a hunter be required to make all calculations mentally? As of yet, the U.S. Fish and Wildlife Service and the 50 state wildlife agencies have passed no regulations prohibiting computers, either pocket-size or warehouse-size. It is up to the individual hunter to do what his conscience dictates. From my own point of view, I see nothing unethical about pocket computers, and I do not hesitate to carry them to the dove field.

In one way of looking at it, successful gunning is relative. If all the gunners in a field get a limit of 12 birds, each hunter is successful. Why get technical about how many shells it took some hunter to fill his card? The only time I ever mention the shells-per-dove ratio is when I happen to get lucky. Then, I tell the other hunters simply to boost their morale by encouraging and inspiring them.

Getting back to the shooting being relative, though, if most of the gunners get seven or eight birds and I get two, then it's an unsuccessful shoot. If I happen to get a limit and no one else does—well, things don't get better than that. That's relativity.

Actually, if the real truth were known, I am not a mathematical shooter, never have been and never will be. I have a birth defect that prevents it. I never believed you could add fractions, or that a minus times a minus equals a plus, or that there was any common sense to income tax forms. I think all this mathematical stuff is a bunch of gibberish made up by high priests to get jobs. I've never known a mathematician in my life who was a good dove shot.

I've found, however, that the theory of mathematical shooting helps my relative dove score in the field. That's one reason I usually carry a pocket computer. When I see some shooter on a hot streak, I walk over and tell him I'm having computer problems and ask him to help. Then, I outline a problem of a dove flying in a crosswind at a ground speed of 43 mph at an altitude of 34 yards with a changing deflection approaching 90 degrees. I ask him to help me work out on the computer just how much I should lead such a shot. I'm quite humble about it.

That interrupts his shooting for several minutes. When he finally gives up, I go back to my stand. I can see his lips moving as the next dove comes in, though, and he shoots 40 feet behind. After he does that a couple times, he gets down on his knees in the sand, takes a stick, and starts figuring. He might as well go back to the car—he's through shooting for the day.

When you start mentally calculating each move while shooting doves, you've had it!

Last dove season, I was invited to a shoot where the guest of honor was a skeet gunner who had won several state championships over the years. Before the shoot, some of the boys were betting on whether he'd limit out in

15 or 20 minutes. I made it a point to ride in the same car with him from town to the field. I took a trigonometry book along that he might be interested in.

The trip seemed a good chance for me to learn a lot about wingshooting, so I asked many pertinent questions. I asked the famous gunner if he had majored in mathematics in college. He said he had taken social sciences. I wondered if he could explain Einstein's theory of relativity as it applied to dove shooting.

He was beginning to look a little uncomfortable so I said, "You must be an expert on Bernoulli's law of physics on airfoils and lift. Do you think studying Bernoulli's works helps with skeet and dove shooting?"

He said he had been meaning to read them but just hadn't gotten around to it.

I asked him a lot of questions about triangulation, deflection, and lag time. I was interested in knowing if he used a special shotshell load and, if so, what was the muzzle velocity and did it ever cause holes in his pattern. I gave him a lot of things to think about.

The host was a wealthy landowner, who was putting on a barbecue after the shoot. He even furnished the shells. When the hotshot skeet shooter reached for a couple of boxes, the landowner said loudly, "Only one box for the expert. Everybody has to stop with 12 birds."

I could see the skeet shooter trying to edge away from me, but I followed and got in a blind next to his. We were early and the doves weren't moving, so I took my trig book over for a visit.

"Say," I said, "I always get mixed up on this sine, cosine, and tangent business. Maybe you could help me before the birds start coming in?"

He readily admitted he didn't know much about trig or the mathematical theory of shooting. That gave me a chance to explain to him some of my theories of mentally calculating each approaching dove as an equation. He was a nice fellow and tried to follow my explanations, but I could see he was becoming more and more confused. I finally went back to my blind when the shooting started down the field. I was sure I had given him a lot to occupy his mind.

The first two birds that came to my blind were hoverers, but I managed to knock them down anyway. I yelled, "Physics and math pay off every time"!

The skeet shooter was having a tough time. He missed six birds straight but managed to hit the seventh. I hollered over, "What angle of deflection did you use?"

There was no reply. I guess the sun was getting in his eyes because he missed the next five. He finally bagged another and then missed four more. He seemed to do a lot of mumbling.

I left him alone after that. There was no way he could get a limit with that one box of shells. He'd have to suffer the humiliation of bumming shells from another shooter or walking back to the starting point where the cases of shells were.

There were plenty of doves and, with a lot of luck, we average powder-burners in the field limited out that afternoon. I never did know for sure how the hot-shot fared. He didn't show up for the post-hunt socializing. Fact is, I never did see him again. That's a shame; I had another mathematical theory of skeet shooting he might have been interested in.

I've found that my theories of dove shooting are helpful on many occasions. I never hesitate to expound them just before a shoot, and if the situation warrants, I may explain them to a gunner right in the middle of a shoot.

One of my closest friends, who is an even worse shot than I, has caught on to the basic value of these theories. He calls them "the old equalizers."

I, Being of Sound Mind

According to lawyers, everyone should make out a will. The main reason is that it might keep your heirs from fighting as much. When you list your hunting gear, your wife also might finally learn the names of all the stuff that has cluttered her home for so many years.

For sentimental reasons, you might prefer that certain items go to old friends outside the family. If you don't legally list the items and specify where you want them to go, though, they are liable to be disposed of at a garage sale or with the trash collector. Recently, at the suggestion of a lawyer, who's a hunting acquaintance, I added a codicil to my will specifying the disposition of my hunting stuff.

Many items, of course, have value only to me because they are reminders of pleasant days afield with old friends. I cannot bequeath their spiritual value, but only their material being.

For instance, I have always had a great sentimental attachment to the mounted caribou head in the garage. My wife never shared my sentiments for it and that may be the reason it never hung inside the home. Because there has never been a keen appreciation for it during my life, there is no reason to believe she would want to maintain it after my departure.

Louise, the wife of my hunting buddy down the street, has long coveted the caribou head. Many a time I've heard her say, "I'd just like to see Bill bring home a head like that!" So I have made Louise the sole beneficiary of the full-cape caribou mount. I know she will enjoy it and take good care of it.

To my lifelong hunting acquaintance Tight-Fist McGuire, I have bequeathed all my reloading tools and whatever ammunition and components are on the premises at my departure, regardless of gauge or caliber. To my knowledge, he has never gone on any type of hunting trip where he didn't scrounge ammo from somebody.

Because it will require effort for Tight-Fist to move the reloading equipment across town to his house, the codicil specifies that up to $150 can be paid from my estate for a moving company to transfer the gear. It also states that preferably the equipment shall be dumped on McGuire's front porch in the dead of night.

To my good friend Angus Lairsey, I leave all my technical books on firearms, ammunition, and gun trading. If Angus has the books, he won't be disturbing my widow in the middle of the night to look up some obscure fact on ballistics. There is one stipulation. If any shooter reports to the executor of my estate that he has heard Angus arguing about the relative merits of a 30/06 cartridge compared with a .308, or any ballistics matter whatsoever, the provision is forfeited and the books shall be given to the county library.

Angus has long lusted for my books and has used them more than I have. I am not leaving the books to Angus for his benefit, though. The bequest is to give all the area's shooters a permanent vacation from Angus's pontification on small ballistical matters that don't make any difference to begin with.

To Midway Ozbolt, one of my dearest wingshooting buddies, I leave a poster embossed with the 100 best excuses for missing a flying bird that I have heard in a lifetime. He is encouraged to use any or all of them. For the past quarter of a century, he has constantly used one general excuse: something was wrong with his gun!

Midway has always implied that if he owned my shotguns, he would seldom or never miss. My will stipulates that Midway is to have first choice of any of my shotguns, the others he is to sell and give the money to the Sheriff's Ranch.

Midway is given full rights to take the shotgun and modify it any way he wants. He can beat on the tang, offcast the stock, raise the comb, ream the choke, or anything else he wants to do to mess up a perfectly good shotgun. There is one stipulation, however. If any wingshooter ever hears Midway say he missed a bird because of the gun he was using, or because he left his best gun at home, my bequeathed shotgun must be passed on to the Sheriff's Ranch.

Thermocline Cowdery has been willed my outdoor clothing, including footwear, with the provision that he can keep for his own use all or any part, provided that any surplus be given to Goodwill, the Salvation Army, or any agency that will take it. Thermocline has long been one of my best deer-hunting companions. But no matter what clothing he wears, he is not comfortable if the temperature drops below 50 degrees F. or if it climbs above 65 degrees.

Because we're about the same size, it is my sincere hope that from his inheritance he will have a wider selection of clothing. In turn, any surviving partners should not have to listen to his complaints about the weather.

The executor of my estate shall take all harmless gadgets that a hunter is likely to collect to the local fire department to be converted into Christmas toys. These shall include, but not be limited to, all game calls, decoys, harmonicas, camouflage greasepaint, tie tacks with hunting themes, flashlights, dog whistles, and humorous gadgets that buddies send when you're sick, provided the latter are clean enough for children.

To Fatback Loudermilk, I bequeath all my camping pots, pans, cutlery, utensils, and collection of seasonings. Fatback, who goes to camp to cook and not to hunt, has never been known to clean any utensils more thoroughly than a quick dip in the nearest creek. The executor of my estate is granted a fund of $100 to have my cookware steamed so that Fatback can start at least one season with clean utensils.

Because Fatback has always wanted my 48-inch-wide sleeping bag, I have willed it to him with one stipulation. He must start the next season by cooking with the utensils bequeathed him, even though they don't have a layer of crud.

The wildlife prints that cover the walls in our home are to be taken by the executor and given back to Ducks Unlimited, the National Wild Turkey Federation, and other organizations that auctioned them. The organizations are to sell them again.

While I'm glad they will profit, the main reason for this provision is to give my wife some relief. I am fully aware that there are art subjects in the world other than wildlife. My wife has told me so many times. This provision of my will opens a lot of wall space and my wife will be free to hang pictures of her ancestors, all of which have been resting uncomfortably in the attic for many years.

Some people are inclined to think that when you make a will it is final. That is not true. As long as you live, you can make any changes or additions you choose. I am sure that I will think of other provisions I wish to add. The main goal, of course, is to think of the welfare of those we leave behind.

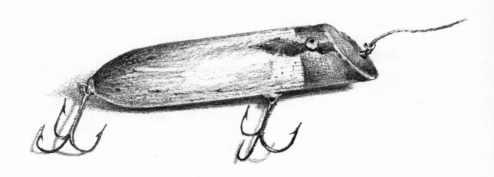

The Awful Truth

Few anglers come back from a fishing trip and talk about not catching anything. In fact, no one is as silent as the fisherman who just got skunked. At least he is quiet about that particular trip. It's not a suitable topic for conversation.

On returning from a trip, which the fish won, experienced fishermen have many stratagems for deflecting pointed questions which probe a tender spot. One common method is for the angler to refuse to talk to anyone for a day or two.

Another strategy to curtail pointed questions is for the angler to put on a big air of modesty. He looks into the distance, secretly smiles, and lowers his head. He may kick a few tufts of grass, glance up, and appear mysterious. He uses body language to imply that while he caught tons of fish, he is too modest to talk about it.

There is another sneaky deflection an angler may use. He hints that he found paradise lost and loaded the boat. He doesn't say how many fish he caught but emphasizes the great number of lures he lost. He may throw in a little technical jargon to give the impression he knows what he's talking about.

What he's doing is laying a trail. He wants you to think he has discovered a secret honeyhole churning with fish. He understands full well that he's not expected to give away the location or any of the details of any fish assembly grounds he's located. If you press him too hard, he may act shocked that you would violate fishing ethics by asking for classified information.

Another way anglers returning from a drubbing change the conversation is to bring up past victories.

When you ask him what he caught, he replies, "Well, I didn't do as well as one day on Big Lake back in 1968. The fish were schooled up and. . . ."

If you don't stop him right there, you may be in for an hour's recitation. There's no time limit on a diversionary tactic, and he'll be glad to relate one successful story after another. If you give him an inch of slack on 1968, he'll remember a trip in 1958 or one in 1978.

You notice how smoothly he deflects your question by saying, "Well, I didn't do as well. . . ." He didn't catch a fish for three days on his recent trip, but palms it off by comparing it with a lucky earlier jaunt. There is a strong implication that his recent trip was at least moderately successful.

An angler with his back to the wall, doesn't hesitate to change the subject. To keep from admitting that he got zipped, he may become philosophical about fishing. That gives him a lot of running room, and by the time he's hung you up on rocks and snags you don't remember what you asked him in the first place.

When you meet a buddy just back from a week's fishing trip, and he starts the conversation by talking about how beautiful the mountains were, you know he didn't catch many fish.

He's trying to get you off on a scenic tour so you won't ask the pointed question of how many fish he caught. If you don't crank on a tight drag, he'll give you the history, culture, and geography for the whole state, including the main farm products. Some anglers develop hearing problems on their trips. You can bluntly ask them what they caught and they'll tell you what they had for breakfast every morning.

I have never understood why fishermen are so afraid to come right out and admit they got clobbered. It is the nature of any sport that sometimes you win and other times you lose. We all understand it.

I mentioned this to my wife during a recent rainy spell as I was reading my diary from a few years back. She asked if she might look at some of the entries over the years.

She flipped the pages and happened to stop at April 1974. Smiling to herself, she combed the days. Then she looked at me and said, "On April 3, 9, 12, 17, 21 and 26 you were skunked. You didn't catch a fish!"

I grabbed the diary from her hands and yelled, "Where does it say that?"

She replied sweetly, "It's all in code. On April 3 you wrote all about the number of song birds and shore birds you saw. That's all!"

I didn't like the gleam in her eye as she continued, "On April 9 you wrote a paragraph about the beautiful sunset, but there's no mention of any fish being caught. It's like that for every day you struck out. You wrote about everything except fish."

"That doesn't prove a thing!" I shouted.

My wife was chuckling. "Well, let's take another look at the entries. On April 4 you recorded in bold writing that you caught five bass, the largest weighing four pounds. I wonder why you didn't mention what the other bass weighed?"

She thumbed down the pages and said, "On April 28 you must have gotten lucky. You have underlined that you caught 15 bluegills on wet flies. There are several paragraphs on weather and water conditions, cover, locations of brushpiles, and references to solunar tables."

My wife paused, then said, "What's this? The last entry must be a note to yourself. 'Go to church Sunday and put extra money in collection plate.'

"Here's your entry for yesterday when you got skunked. Let's see what it says. My, my, that must have been a wonderful orange and purple sunset ! It's all you wrote about!"

I mumbled something about an orange and purple sunset being code and she didn't understand that there's more to fishing than just catching a fish.

She shook her head, "You fishermen are really something! You won't even admit it to yourselves when you get skunked, not even to your diary."

Never Say Diet

A lot of people—wives, for example—don't understand how a hunter can go to camp for three days and gain five pounds.

Well, part of the reason is the law of over-compensation. Hunters know they will be using a lot of energy climbing hills, cutting firewood, and dragging trophy deer out of the woods. So when hunters shop for camp supplies, they lean toward high starch foods such as potatoes, macaroni, and pancake flour.

Hunters gravitate toward ham and steaks circumscribed by layers of fat. Packaged foods that are easy to prepare are usually high in calories. If someone took cabbage to camp, it would be fried in grease.

Fresh air and outdoor living do something to a hunter's appetite, namely bring out the glutton. The first morning at camp, a hunter eats three eggs, five pieces of sausage, and a pint of syrup on hot biscuits. Then, someone drives him to his deer stand where he sits staring at the scenery for three hours.

Around 10 a.m., he is picked up and driven back to camp. He's so hungry he can't wait for lunch and eats two sweet rolls. Before noon, he's taken in 4,000 calories and used maybe 100 if he grunted real hard getting in and out of the Jeep. Most of the 100 calories used were expended during his struggle to get into his hunting britches and trying to see his belt buckle.

Dinner mortgages his quota of calories for the next week. The hunter has walked a total of 500 yards all day and is famished. After that strenuous exercise, he tells himself that he deserves a good meal to rebuild his muscle tissue. He has earned a reward.

I have never been to a deer camp where the larder contained lettuce, carrots, celery, yogurt, and other low-calorie foods. With guns around, no one has the nerve to show up with fresh fruit and protein bread.

Peanut butter-and-jelly sandwiches are staples for camp snacks. After all, a hunter has to keep his energy up. You use up a lot of energy every time it's your turn to deal.

My wife puts me on strict diets between hunting camps. She says that if I reach the end of the hunting season without gaining weight, it's a moral victory.

I buy every diet book that comes on the market. I keep looking for one that tells you how to eat all you want without gaining weight. None of the books work. Recently, I bought one called *How Fat Hunters Can Turn Skinny Without Suffering*. It explained how to fast. The headaches and pains go away after the first 48 hours, if you survive.

Another book is titled *How To Be A Skinny Glutton*. You eat all you want on Christmas Day each leap year, but the rest of the time you're on yogurt and water.

Another book is called *Getting Thin Through Grease*. You can eat all the grease you want for three meals a day—you just can't mix or spread it with other food. After a month of straight grease, most of your stomach is removed.

One popular diet book is titled *Don't Let Eating Interfere With Your Drinking*. What you do is go on a liquid diet. When you reach malnutrition, the weight just peels off. If scurvy strikes, you add lime juice.

Half the hunters in America are toting around calorie-count cards. They swap them like bubblegum cards. Eveyone is looking for a secret formula that requires no effort.

A fat hunting friend of mine in the printing business designs his own cards. One says, "Chocolate Cookies Have No Calories." Another reads, "Apple Pie Is Low Calorie Unless You Add The Second Scoop Of Ice Cream." He's his own best customer. Because the slogan is in print, it must be true. Everybody in town is trying to get his cards. A local songwriter has cut a record called, "Printing Man, We Love You."

Actually, anyone who is sincere about dieting doesn't need calorie cards. All that is necessary is to follow a few basic rules. If you do, you can safely eat at any hunting camp in the world without fear of gaining weight:

1. If it tastes good, don't eat it.

2. If you crave it, forget it.

3. If it's sweet or greasy, you shouldn't have it.

4. If it will give you a satisfying feeling, don't touch it.

5. If eating it will improve your disposition, don't.

6. If it will give you energy, it's bad for you.

7. If it smells good, it has too many calories.

8. If you frequently dream about it, don't go near it, not even just to fondle.

There are certain common exercises that one may indulge in at camp for hours, but they burn up few calories. For instance, telling hunting stories until the early hours of the morning mainly exercises only the jawbones. Wildly gesturing with the hands uses a minimum of calories. Getting up from one's chair to freshen a potable with ice does not require much energy.

About the only sure way I know to lose weight at camp is to get lost the first day. You eat all your candy bars during the first hour just to calm your nerves. For the next three days, you live on survival food such as roots and dried berries. Believe me, eating roots will take the pounds off. But remember when you finally walk out of the woods you'll be entitled to a big meal.

Deceived by the Ringusdingus

Y ou could never ask for a better hunting camp partner than Quintus Perkins. The only trouble was he had this thing about shooting does. Like the rest of us, he remembered when deer were as scarce as volunteers to talk to the Garden Club on potting wild violets.

That was back when a doe was sacred. Anybody who shot a doe was so low he had to wear stilts to walk under a snake's belly. It was worse than shooting a robin on the ground in the preacher's front yard. Much worse! There were plenty of robins but the whitetails seemed slow in bouncing back.

At least it seemed slow to our Buck, Gourmet, and Classical Poetry Club. I'm sure it seemed that way to hunters in other regions, too, but suddenly the deer caught on to the multiplication game. In a few years, they seemed to explode, even on our leased property.

Now the state game department was going around saying to sportmen, "Boys, we got to shoot some of those does. The herd is beyond the carrying capacity of the food, and they're eating themselves out of house and home. On top of that, the sex ratio between does and bucks is out of kilter. If we cut down on some of the does, there'll be room for more bucks."

A biologist came out and we drove him around our lease for a couple of days and did some jacklighting at night. He showed us the high browse line and pointed out how skinny our does and fawns were. Then he asked, "How many bucks did you see?"

We realized what the biologist was telling us was true, but sometimes it takes an outside expert to get things in focus. He gave us 10 red doe tags for the coming season, one for each member. The does had to be shot in fair chase during the regular hunting season and immediately tagged. If a hunter didn't want to use his tag, he could give it to a guest or another member.

Everybody thought it was a good system except Quintus. He said he wasn't going to shoot a doe, not even to save his life if one charged him. What's more, he wasn't going to eat any doe at camp that someone else shot.

We have a rickety old camp with a wood stove inside and a grill on the back porch where we can charcoal broil with a few wet hickory chips, smoking just enough to add a little outdoor flavor. When the season opened last fall, I drew the job of cooking the first night. I had it rigged that way.

Quintus made a big deal of presenting me his red doe tag the night before and said that I was welcome to any more tags that ever came his way.

It was like a Chinese fire drill when the alarm clock went off the first morning. I was rushing the coffee, biscuits and ham, and old Quintus wanted to know why I had on my hunting clothes. He said, "After we're gone, you can shoot a doe from the front yard."

Well, I know better than that. It's true you see plenty of does when you don't want to but when you're anxious to shoot one, they disappear like the bucks.

Anyway, I was lucky that morning and shot a 1 ½-year-old doe that had gotten fat on acorns and corn. I took her back to camp and butchered out the steaks.

What everyone in camp knew except Quintus was that I had a Kansas City strip steak that had cost me about a day's pay. I carefully cut it into slices the same size as the doe steaks.

If you look closely; it's easy to tell the difference. Venison is not marbled with fat. The fat accumulates in certain places, such as the rump but it is not ingrained in the lean. A good steak is marbled with fat throughout the lean. The fat is what makes it so tender and juicy.

When the hunters came in after dark, they were starving and a little bourbon and branchwater was enough of a whetstone for them to chew through the wooden table. I started serving venison steaks, baked potatoes, and spinach souffle to everyone except Quintus. Then I told him I had the ringusdingus cut from the doe saved for him.

I brought him a couple slabs of that steak and told him to try just one bite. If he didn't like it, I'd fix him up a bowl of oatmeal. Well, old Quintus had nine people looking at him and he was hungry! He cut off a tiny sliver and tasted it. Then he cut off a bigger chunk and gulped it down. Then he dropped his knife and said, "Boys, this is so tender you can cut it with a fork."

After he cleaned up the two slabs, I brought him in the last two still warming on the grill. He gulped them down like an old hound being thrown hushpuppies. When he finally finished, he pushed back from the table and said, "Boys, that's the best venison I ever had in my life. I'd like to get my red deer tag back."

I gave him mine. A week or so later, he dropped a big doe and took it home and hung it for a week, the way venison should be handled. The night he decided to butcher it, he invited friends for dinner. He phoned me about 10 p.m. and said how much everyone enjoyed the venison dinner. He paused and said, "I've got just one question. When you're cutting up a doe, just where is the ringusdingus? I never could find it in mine."

A Dog-Eat-Bird World

Bird dogs are basically selfish. They'd rather do what they want to do than what their owner wants them to do. Bird dogs, like some hunters, have too much ego. They think they know what they're doing all the time. At the very least, they think the way they want to do things is the only way.

The character traits of self-will and ego are reflected in a dog's attitude and behavior. If you don't believe it, just think back to any time you have let a dog out of a hunting vehicle in a strange place. The first thing the dog does is spray every bush in sight.

The dog doesn't go into his hydraulic act because it's been a long time between rest stops or because he has short kidneys. The bush ceremony is the method by which a dog stakes his territory. With the act of irrrigation, he claims the turf as his own.

I realize this is traditional and accepted behavior in the dog world, but to me the ceremony reflects a bad attitude. The dog doesn't care who already owns the territory, looks after it, and pays taxes on it. He doesn't make any attempt to find out if the land is already under private ownership, nor does he care. For all the dog knows, the territory could be under Chapter 11 of the bankruptcy laws with many claimants disputing rights to the land. A bird dog's system solves a lot of legal red tape in a hurry. He cocks his leg, goes through his ceremony, and the land is now his. He's ready for the next case.

Although this may be normal behavior for a bird dog, this flippant attitude creates problems in relationships with owners. No matter how much you do for a bird dog, he always assumes he knows more about hunting than you do.

Getting a bird dog to do what you want him to do when you want him to is called "breaking a dog." It has been my experience that bird dogs break more hunters than hunters break bird dogs. Dogs break hunters physically, mentally, spiritually, morally, and sometimes financially.

Just when you think you have a dog fully broke, he'll embarrass you with some behavior he's never exhibited before. It will always be in front of a hunter you are trying to impress. For instance, your boss, for the first time in his life, gets a double on a flushing covey of bobwhite quail. Your pointer, which has faultlessly retrieved all season, runs to the first bird and picks it up. The pointer turns toward you, looks you both in the eye, and then swallows the quail whole in one gulp. Before you can recover, the pointer grabs the second bird, tosses it into the air like a peanut, catches it in his mouth, and swallows it in one smooth motion. In fact, the descending quail loses no velocity until it is suddenly halted by the pointer's stomach.

The dog does not swallow the quail because he is hungry. He does not eat them for the taste because they do not remain in his mouth long enough for him to taste them. He eats the quail as another reminder of who is really running the show.

On any given hunt, when a bird dog does everything perfectly in front of other hunters, the odds are astronomical that the dog will never repeat the performance. The biggest favor you can do yourself is get affidavits in triplicate and retire the dog to stud.

Recently I went hunting with Ed Norman, who operates Quailridge Plantation down in Norman Park, Georgia. I like to hunt with Ed because he is patient, which is what you have to be if you operate a hunting preserve for the public.

Ed was kind enough to let me bring my two setters, Long Gone Sam, now nine, and Rat, son of Long Gone Sam. Rat is three years old but he may not live much longer. He might run himself to death chasing missed quail.

Long Gone has slowed down a bit with age. He runs faster than he can for the first hour, but then slows to wide open. He has always had a secretive streak. He likes to hunt someplace where you can't see him, such as three miles away. After he put a claim on Ed's Jeep wheels, he lost interest in local territory and decided to invest in foreign lands.

Ed is a good Christian man and if he can find something nice to say about your dog, he will say it. We hadn't been hunting with Rat for much more than three hours when Ed said, "Rat sure has good teeth."

If you think about it, it does take pretty good teeth for a dog to bite a hole in a mud-grip tire. Maybe Rat wasn't happy about Long Gone putting a prior claim on the Jeep.

After Long Gone disappeared in one of the adjoining counties, Rat managed to indicate where a single quail was hiding. It was not a stylish point, one reason being that Rat lay flat on his stomach. At least his head was staunch and pointed in the right direction. Ed said for me not to get upset because Rat is still in the puppy stage. I took that as a polite way of saying Rat is short in the mental department.

Rat thought it was cute to point from a prone position and did it again with the next single. I could see at the rate he was going I'd soon own the only setter in the country that rolled over on his back to point with all four feet extended toward heaven.

It was not an ideal time to try and sell my dogs to Ed, but I told him if he'd take them I'd throw in my automobile to boot. Ed said the kindest thing he could—that my two dogs showed a certain amount of promise. He'd give a lot to own them, but their color didn't match his kennel scheme.

Fortunately, Ed had along a couple of his pointers that were recently weaned. He put them down and in an hour or so I had my day's quota of quail. I asked Ed if he thought my setters learned anything by watching his pointer pups. Ed said he was positive they did but, to be honest, my dogs seemed to have more natural talent for staking territory than for locating bobwhite quail.

Parlez-vous Fishing?

Sportsmen sometimes complain that they are misunderstood by normal people. Well, one of the reasons is that hunters and fishermen use a great deal of jargon and semitechnical talk. There's not only a communication gap but a total collapse. Sometimes sportmen can't even understand each other.

Take the word speck. A speck can be a crappie, a saltwater trout, a speckle-bellied goose, a brook trout, any object at a distance which looks small, or something which gets in your eye. It can also mean a quantity, such as, "I'll take a speck of that venison stew."

A speck also can mean a linear distance. For instance, a hunter might say, "The deer was standing at 1,000 yards, and I shot a speck under him." That could mean anything from the bullet hitting between the buck's legs to the bullet kicking up dirt 100 yards short.

Depending on regional use, speck can mean guess, imagine, or assume. As an example, an angler might say, "I 'speck I'll go fishing in the morning."

Speck is a popular name for pointers, setters, Brittany spaniels, and other hunting breeds likely to be speckled in coloring against a white background. It's a handy name for a dog because it has only one syllable, and it's easy to shout when your dog is running off and not paying attention to you. It's also a fairly common name for male humans who are inclined to be fair skinned and carry around a lot of freckles. I have never heard a female person called Speck, but it is common to say of one, "She's as cute as a speckled pup."

Fishermen use the term speck to describe distance. For example, an angler might say, "That bass missed my plug a speck." In certain regions the term denotes time. A fisherman might say, "The bass hit at my buzzbait a speck late."

There's no end of things that the word speck might or might not mean. For instance, "I was looking over the gunwale at some bluegills and my specks fell off." That does not refer to freckles, but spectacles.

Sportsmen must have run short of words when developing a vocabulary, or perhaps there's something appealing about the word speck. For instance, an angler might turn up a container of refreshments and then shake his head and say, "There's not a speck left."

How in the world can earth people or a wife know what a sportsman is talking about?

In much of the rural South, the largemouth bass is called a trout or green trout. City anglers use the term largemouth bass. The strange part is that the largemouth bass is not a true bass at all but a sunfish.

If civilians think that's confusing, the buglemouth bass is not either a bass or a sunfish. It's a carp!

The brook or mountain trout is not a trout but a char. A rainbow trout that leaves freshwater and goes to sea becomes a steelhead upon its return.

I suppose every sport develops its own language. Golfers seem proud when they shoot an eagle. Don't they know eagles are an endangered species and protected by law? They also brag about shooting birdies. It always sounds to me as if they've done something illegal such as clobbering a tweetie bird.

It's no wonder that the general public doesn't understand much about hunting and fishing. Who but a dog man would know that a gyp is a female dog and a riprap a canine with a basic white coat dotted with a lot of black specks?

A business friend of mine recently considered modernizing his office by adding computers. The first thing the computer company did was send him to school for a week to learn the special computer language. Then he could understand what they were talking about and could make a decision on the best model for his needs.

Maybe that's what the wives and young kids of sportsmen need. They could go to school and learn outdoor terminology. When the husband asked where his wife had moved his fly rod, she wouldn't bring him a flipping stick.

Sportsmen know that a 21 is a side-by-side shotgun, a 70 is a rifle which comes in several calibers, and an XP-100 is a target pistol. How in the world would a wife or kid know that? In the first place, the numbering system doesn't make any sense. Even the sportsman wonders why a lot of numbers in between were skipped over.

If you think sportsmen's jargon is simple, try explaining choke, pattern, and gauge to your wife. In fact, try explaining choke to a hunter. Or, try explaining to yourself why the .244 caliber rifle didn't sell well, but when they changed the name of the rifle to 6mm it became popular.

There is one advantage to the mixed-up way cartridges got their designations over the years. If your wife wants to take up hunting, but you're not really in favor of it, tell her the first step is to learn the names of all the centerfire cartridges which are interchangeable, the various bullet weights, the ballistics of each, and the advantages and disadvantages of each caliber. That'll send her back to her sewing circle. In fact, if I had to do it, I'd probably take up trying to knock little round balls into holes with different choked clubs.

The names of fishing lures are almost as complicated and have about the same amount of logic. Anyone connected with a fishing company, or any inhabitant of a funny farm, can name a lure. In fact, anyone in the whole world can invent a fly and call it whatever he wants to as long as it has no relationship to the basic purpose of the fly.

Even a sportsman in the business has trouble keeping up with the nomenclature. I was fishing with a friend last summer and he told me not to land on a nearby island.

When I asked him the reason, he said, "Ricky lives there."

Well, I didn't know who Ricky was. I looked and looked but I couldn't see any house or even a shack. Finally, I asked who or what Ricky was.

He said, "You know, man. Ricky Rattler."

My heart goes out to anyone trying to learn to interpret sportsmen's talk. Sometimes I think it'd be easier to learn to speak Russian.